CHANGING CAREERS
AFTER 40:

Real Stories, New Callings

by

Terry Pile and David Lingle

ISBN: 978-1-6094402-3-7

Restart Enterprises LLP
www.restartenterprises.com
restartenterprises@gmail.com

Designed, printed, and bound by Vladimir Verano
at Third Place Press, Lake Forest Park,
on the Espresso Book Machine v.2.2.
thirdplacepress.com

Dedicated to
Harvey and Bobbie Nagle
Role Models Extraordinaire
And
George W. Davis
For his inspiration

Acknowledgements

Many thanks to Molly Woolbright for her wise editing, Clare Meeker for her encouragement and advice, Diane Fisch for her thoughtful research, Florence Karnofsky for her judicious insights and the 50+ career changers we interviewed for sharing their stories.

Table of Contents

INTRODUCTION: Starting Over

SECTION I: Forced to Leave

Chapter I: Harvey – Turning a Survival Job into a Career
Turning "just a job" into a rewarding career

Chapter II: John – Creating a Portfolio Career
Developing multiple income streams to satisfy numerous interests

Chapter III: Jeff – The Risky Business of Career Transition
Taking calculated risk for career transition

Chapter IV: David – A New Career with Help from Uncle Sam
Using available resources to launch a new career

SECTION II: Needing to Leave

Chapter V: Marilyn – Focusing on Positive Choices
Creating an extraordinary life

Chapter VI: Robert – Turning Life Lessons into a Career
Impact of raising children on career choices

Chapter VII: Peter – Family Influence on Career Choices
Overcoming expectations and emotional barriers

Chapter VIII: Larissa – Visualizing a New Career
The power of visualization in forming a new career

SECTION III: Compelled to Leave

Chapter IX: Jean – Choosing a Career to Make a Difference
Applying old skills in a new way for the greater good

Chapter X: Janet – From Passion to Paycheck
Turning a hobby into a career

Chapter XI: Gail – Creating a Network of Support
Using new media and old fashion networking to build a new career

Chapter XII: Sharon – The Art of Reinvention
The many sides of self-expression

EPILOGUE

INTRODUCTION:

Starting Over

WHY YOU WILL WANT TO READ THIS BOOK

This is a book about opportunities, how to recognize them when they present themselves and how to open your mind and heart to pursuing them. *Changing Careers after 40: Real Stories, New Callings* is a collection of personal stories of ordinary people with successful careers who were forced or inspired to start over. They are PhDs and high school drop outs, CEOs and blue collar workers, logical thinkers and impetuous do-ers. Some were forced out of their jobs by office politics or a failing economy. Others left because of health or family issues. Many experienced career ennui or the desire to find work that made a difference in the lives of others. All are over 40 years of age and were accomplished in the careers they worked hard to establish. Each left that career to start over.

Today, with a volatile economy and people living longer, healthier lives, employees can no longer expect to stay with one employer or career for an entire working lifetime. That particular paradigm is fading as fast as companies close, merge, restructure, downsize, rightsize, 'consultanize' and outsource. A recent study by AARP claimed 57 percent of workers 45 years and older were delaying retirement or returning to the work-force for economic reasons. Currently, about 17 percent of the workforce is 65 years or older and that number is expected to grow considerably. In a study published in 2008 by the Bureau of Labor Statistics, 65 percent of the workers who started a job between the ages of 38 and 45 changed jobs again within five years.

The changing nature of how companies do business is forcing us to change the way we think about being employees as well. Whether we leave a career willingly or unintentionally, most of us will come to a point in our work life where we have to make a decision about what we want to do next. That's where this book comes in. The individuals portrayed here are role models for anyone, at any age, considering a change to a new vocation. We believe you can learn "how it is done" from their stories.

HOW THIS BOOK CAME TO BE

Terry: As a career counselor, I am frequently approached by people well into mid-life trying to decide, "What next?" Most have successful careers but, for whatever reason, they are ready to move on and do something else. Having had three very different careers myself (first as a school teacher, then as a marketing executive and now as a career counselor), I can empathize with the range of emotions that accompany such a change. The fear of failing, the frustration in finding a compelling career path and the elation in envisioning a new life for oneself are just a few of the conflicting feelings career changers struggle with.

Most clients that come to see me want a quick fix… "Just tell me what to do." Unfortunately, remaking one's professional self isn't a matter of losing a few pounds, buying a trendy wardrobe and getting a new hair style. Some counselors offer a battery of personality tests, interest inventories and exercises promoting introspection and then come up with a list of professions for the client to explore. Generally, their clients are disappointed with this approach when the epiphany doesn't materialize. There is no "quick fix" to guiding potential career changers through the complex process of a career transition.

One rainy December evening, I was in my office waiting for my next client. It was rush hour so I was sure he would be late. A few years ago, I had helped David Lingle secure a management position for a company that developed software for the healthcare industry. Reviewing his file, I was curious as to how he was doing in this role and why he wanted to meet with me.

David arrived exactly on time wearing his signature gray newsboy cap that gave him a jaunty, puckish look, but his tone was serious. "I want to make a career change," he said. "I don't want to work in another technology job. I want to find something more meaningful, something with purpose. How do others do it?"

I could have pulled out my Myers Briggs personality assessment, scheduled another meeting and dismissed this client with his homework. But I knew that wouldn't work with David, who was skeptical about standardized assessments. As I was puzzling over which career change methodology to pursue, it was David who came up with an intriguing proposal for approaching his career transition.

David: At the time I came to see Terry, I was a software development manager. My company recently laid off 60 percent of its engineering team. I knew my turn was coming. A few years ago I earned an MBA and since then had been thinking about the possibility of a career change. I just didn't know what I wanted to do or how to go about it. I had taken the traditional career assessments in the past, but believed they were for young people just entering the job market. They didn't seem to address my needs. Then it occurred to me that many others had been in my situation. I could find people who had successfully changed careers, talk to them and find out how they did it. I also knew that I would need professional help with this project, someone with an understanding of the career change process and contacts that I could talk to. Terry was the perfect person to ask, and she accepted.

Terry and David: Each night we would talk over Skype, discussing our vision and strategies and making lists of potential career changers we wanted to talk to. On weekends, we plied ourselves with coffee as we interviewed career changers in various coffee shops around the Puget Sound. Later we expanded our quest to include career changers around the country, conducting three-way interviews by phone. We asked open ended questions and tried not to influence the conversation. This was to be the career changer's story.

The subjects we selected were individuals who had left established careers and transitioned successfully into new ones. Their success was not measured by money or prestige, but rather by personal satisfaction. We also chose to focus on people 40 years of age and older. Our thinking was it takes several years to establish oneself in a career and once entrenched it becomes much harder to start over. Older workers are particularly vulnerable. If they don't keep skills updated and stay abreast of new trends, changing careers is especially difficult.

Over the course of a year and a half, we interviewed over fifty career changers, many two and three times, digging deeper with each meeting hoping to discover the secret ingredients to making a satisfying career transition. Some of the stories made us laugh, while others moved us to tears. But throughout, we were impressed by the courage, thoughtfulness and perseverance these individuals demonstrated in their pursuit for a more fulfilling work life.

Each of the twelve case studies we eventually selected for this book represent a unique theme or strategy that captures the essence of the career changer's experience. For example, Janet focused on how she could make a career out of a hobby. Harvey discovered that the job he took just to survive could lead to a viable and satisfying career. John came to the realization that he would need multiple income streams to obtain the kind of job security he was seeking and created a "portfolio career." At the end of each story, we expand on the theme by offering end notes in which Terry provides practical "how-to" advice for career changers from a career counselor's perspective. David researched available resources for each theme to assist anyone contemplating the act of making a career transition. As a result, we offer a rainbow of career transition scenarios, strategies and tools to assist a wide spectrum of personalities seeking new vocations.

WHY SUCCESSFUL PEOPLE START OVER: Triggering Events

If you worked hard to build a successful career, why would you want to start over? Although each situation was unique for the career changers we interviewed, there was an event in each person's life that required them to make a change. We categorized these incidents into three broad groups which we labeled "triggering events." These triggering events include:

- Forced out: Leaving due to outside forces
- The Wake-up Call: Leaving because of family or health reasons
- Following Your Heart: Leaving of one's own free will

Regardless of the circumstances, each career changer was successfully established in a profession, experienced a triggering event, and decided to begin anew.

FUNDAMENTALS FOR STARTING OVER: What we Learned

Changing careers is a process. Regardless of the triggering event, successful career changers experience similar steps in the process, with varying degrees of intensity. We identified four significant phases in the career change process:

- Being open to change
- Feeling confused about next steps
- Creating a positive environment
- Showing a willingness to take a risk

Some career changers travel through each phase quickly. Others stumble or get stuck. But through each step of the process, they gain valuable insights that allow them to move closer to finding a new vocation.

Being open to change

The end of a career, whether forced or self-induced, requires a period of mourning. Similar to the death of a loved one, career changers experience varying degrees of anger, fear, sadness and self-doubt. After working through these powerful emotions, all eventually reach a stage of acceptance and are ready to move forward. Jeff was angry at his Board of Directors for their lack of support. Marilyn briefly denounced God for her cancer and Peter blamed his father for his career choice. After working through their feelings, they were ready for positive change and open to exploring new opportunities.

Unfortunately, not everyone can work through these stages of grief effectively. Some get stuck for years in the anger or self-doubt mode resulting in poor career choices. They are either paralyzed by their emotions and find excuses not to look for work, yearn for the good old days, or often return to a similar job because it is "what they know" not "what they want."

What is exciting for us to discover through these case studies, is that once an individual does open his/her mind and heart to change, opportunities start to present themselves. Whether you call it serendipity or luck, those who accept or embrace change are more sensitive to the signs around them, more willing to consider the possibilities. They make statements such as, "I was in the right place at the right time," or "Perhaps it was a coincidence, but…" Although many people we interviewed felt they found their new careers by chance, it was clear to us that they had made their own luck by virtue of being open-minded and willing to explore opportunities, no matter how unlikely they appeared at first glance.

Feeling confused about next steps

Each career changer struggles with the question, "What next?" For some this period of confusion lasts a few weeks; for others, several years. This period of career chaos is inevitable. It creates (or forces) the career changer to explore options, reactivate networks and test the waters. There are false starts and a few failures. But in each case, the career changer finds a way through these obstacles. Harvey was willing to try anything to pay the bills and ended up in a few dead-end jobs. John almost bought a bakery in New England but backed out at the eleventh hour. Janet knew her next career would involve one of her many hobbies, but would it involve gardening, photography or animals? By accepting that a period of uncertainty is part of the career transition process, the act of change becomes more purposeful, an exciting part of exploring new possibilities.

Creating a positive environment

The successful career changer needs to have a strong network of support. It can be a spouse, friends, co-workers, classmates and/or mentors who provide encouragement, positive energy and in some cases, permission to take the leap. Career changers need to make a conscious effort to separate themselves from the negative people or unpleasant activities in their lives. This is particularly difficult if the negative energy comes from family members or close friends, who can become a hindrance to moving forward.

When Marilyn discovered she had cancer, she made a decision to eliminate the negatives in her life. She said "no" to the activities and people who gave her no joy and she received tremendous energy from the positive people she wrapped around herself like a blanket. Jeff's wife presented him with a journal and encouraged him to focus on the kind of work life he wanted to create for himself. Peter found the supportive family he craved among his classmates and teachers when he returned to graduate school.

Ultimately, we must all walk the career path on our own. But it is easier if the path is cleared of negative obstacles and there are a few friendly guides along the way.

Showing a willingness to take a risk

Foremost in our research, we found that successful career changers are willing to take risks. Those who are more risk averse take longer to make the transition and are far more cautious in their approach and planning, but to make the transition, ultimately some level of risk is involved.

For some, like Jeff, risk taking was a predominant theme in his career path. For Harvey, it was imperative to survive. But in each case, the career changer has to be willing to trod new territory and overreach the boundaries of their comfort level for change to occur.

HOW TO USE THIS BOOK

If you are considering a career change, then you have already taken the first step by reading this book. These stories of successful career changers will inspire your desire for a career that is personally satisfying. They will boost your confidence in making a change and excite your thinking as to the possibilities. The end notes at the completion of each narrative focus on a central theme or strategy for changing careers. It provides practical guidelines for navigating change and suggested resources that will help you to focus your research. Most importantly, this book will reassure you that there is very little difference between obstacles and opportunities once you are open to change.

In some instances, names and places have been changed to protect privacy and the circumstances of interviewees may have changed at the time of publication.

SECTION I: FORCED TO LEAVE
Leaving due to outside forces

There are many reasons why people lose their jobs that are beyond their control—poor economic conditions, office politics, financial misman-agement. There are few things more demoralizing than losing one's job, especially when performance is not an issue. When you lose a job you love, it hurts even more because you are vested emotionally as well as financially. You are not just losing a source of income; you are also los-ing friends, structure, purpose, identity. Harvey Nagle, John Curley, Jeff Levy, and David Sherman fell into this category.

After being nudged out of the family business, Harvey became a successful restaurateur until the economy soured and he was forced to declare bankruptcy. In his mid-fifties, having lost his business, house and life savings, Harvey had to start over.

John also found himself faced with the question, "What next?" after his fourteen-year career as a popular television talk show host abruptly ended when the station owners decided not to renew his contract.

Jeff moved up the corporate ladder until he became COO of a mul-timillion-dollar company. Thinking he would remain there until retire-ment, he unexpectedly found himself back on the street, unemployed and considering his career options.

David too had to face the prospect of starting over, after being forced out of his decades-long career in the jewelry business due to a tepid market.

CHAPTER I:

Harvey Nagle - Turning a Survival Job Into a Career

Harvey Nagle didn't experience the traditional "one career for a lifetime" approach as many others did of his generation. He became a career changer long before it was fashionable. Twice he was forced out of careers he thought would see him through to retirement. Through a string of unfortunate occurrences and a few bad decisions, Harvey ended up in jobs he never imagined for himself. Perseverance and his willingness to take any work to survive allowed him to discover innate skills and strengths that he parlayed into a third career from which, now in his retirement years, he is still reaping benefits.

An early 1960s photograph of Harvey Nagle shows an imposing figure in a white butcher's coat with rows of beef carcasses hanging from meat hooks in the background. Thick, gray-rimmed glasses give him a bold, cocky look. Nagle is confidently posing in the meat cooler of his family's slaughter house and meat packing plant in Lansing, Illinois. At age thirty-eight, he is clearly King of the Cooler, prepared to face any challenge that comes his way.

Harvey started working at sixteen, long before his peers, dropping out of school in 1942 to help in the family meat packing plant. With his father and older brother, Mickey, he helped Nagle Packing grow from a small operation to one that employed over 100 people and slaughtered 3,000 animals a week. He learned a lot about running an animal hide cellar, hiring and supervising people, working with suppliers and selling meat and animal byproducts. "We had a comfortable life style," Nagle recalls. "The pay wasn't great but there were a lot of perks."

As the company grew, so too did the tension between Harvey and his older brother. Mickey had gained status as the favored son, gradually assuming greater control over the business and pushing his younger brother into the background while diminishing his responsibilities. After twenty-plus years working at Nagle Packing, Harvey reluctantly accepted Mickey's offer to buy his share of the company. He was forty-two and, for the first time since he was a teenager, unemployed.

On a blustery weekend in November, with cash in the bank but no plan, Harvey took cover in a B. Dalton bookstore during a drenching rainstorm. Drying out among the best sellers and business books, he read a book on franchising. It was the start of his riches to rags journey.

"I was in my early forties and scared to be on my own. After being pushed out of the family business, I lacked confidence in myself and a franchise seemed to be the right way for me to go." Harvey bought a Mr. Steak franchise based on the fact that he "knew meat" and a little bit about the restaurant business from Nagle Packing's customers. He believed the company had a successful formula and good track record. They would provide him with the expertise, training and marketing he needed to get the restaurant going.

The first five years in business were prosperous ones. Harvey and his wife, Bobbie, frequently talked about retiring to a house on the beach in Florida. With a custom home under construction, a new Mercedes in the garage and three kids just about out of college, Harvey decided to open a second restaurant.

It was the early 1980s when the contractor broke ground, the same time the country was sinking in to a major recession that was considered to be the most serious since the Great Depression. High inflation forced the Federal Reserve to slow the growth of the money supply and increase interest rates. By June of 1982, prime interest rates had reached 20 percent. Caught off guard by crippling overhead, increased competition and poor management decisions, Harvey was in a free fall. At the age of fifty-eight, the once successful entrepreneur had lost two restaurants, his car, home and life savings. "I remember my thirty-fifth wedding anniversary clearly. Bobbie and I were at a Venture store, celebrating with the $1.50 polish hot dog and soda special. That's all we could afford. We were really in bad shape financially. It was very scary."

This time Harvey was facing unemployment without the benefit of a financial safety net. He also didn't have the luxury to be discriminating. He tried to get any job he could find to pay off his growing debt, including sales jobs with car dealers and furniture stores, but met with little success. In the 1980s, these industries tended to hire young, high energy, fast talking sales people. Harvey Nagle didn't fit the bill.

"The best motivation for finding a job is being hungry and I was willing to try anything." Harvey attended career seminars, read classified ads and did a lot of networking. For a time, he took a job as a courier driving at all hours within a fifty-mile radius of Chicago. Occasionally he found opportunities to work as a broker selling meat to former customers of the meat packing plant. He also took a job as a fence salesman for Montgomery Ward. Even though he wasn't a fast talker, he found that he enjoyed sales and excelled at it. He was a good listener who easily gained peoples' trust and he enjoyed the interaction with customers, never daunted by rejection. His success at Montgomery Ward gave him the confidence to look for more lucrative work in sales, an area he felt played to his strengths.

Through his brother-in-law's connections, Harvey eventually landed a job with Jumbo Box and Paper Company selling custom boxes and paper products to an eclectic group of clients, from furriers to bakeries and advertising agencies. The job came with a boss who had excellent experience in the industry as well as a reputation for being a tyrant. "No one mentioned that there had been sixteen sales people before me. None of them stayed. But me, I needed the job."

At 6:00 a.m. each morning, Harvey was required to report to Paul Donnelly by phone to review his plan for the day. The process was repeated before he went home at night. Never sure whether he would be berated or praised, Harvey complied. In spite of his boss's boot camp management style, Harvey realized he was getting an invaluable sales education from Paul. "I learned more from him than anyone else in my life, but he was brutal."

Determined not to let Paul beat him down, Harvey found that his enthusiasm for the "box business" was starting to grow. He was able to apply his aptitude for sales, frequently cold calling new clients. He knew how to be persistent and handle rejection. He also enjoyed troubleshooting and problem solving with his customers. Harvey kept an eagle eye on the competition; he knew their prices and had a good sense for how much he could discount and still make a profit.

At age sixty-five, Harvey had been in the paper products industry for six years. By that time, Paul was ancient history and Jumbo had gone out of business. Harvey now had a job with Hero Container Company as a package goods broker with a much broader inventory. He had over 100 accounts and was making an excellent income earning 50% commission and, ironically, beginning to get calls from headhunters. "All of a sudden I was marketable. I had something everyone wanted — accounts." Harvey had created his own definition of a master salesman.

Now in his eighties, Harvey is financially secure and has allowed himself to slow down a bit. Although the beach house in Florida never materialized, he seems content with his mid-west lifestyle. Most days he is at home with Bobbie, reading novels, tending his lawn or baking cookies with his black cocker, Maggie, by his side waiting for a stray crumb. He no longer makes the sixty-mile drive each way to the Hero Container Company. Nevertheless, he is still writing off his home office as a business expense and receiving modest commission checks in the mail from the loyal accounts he continues to nurture. He laughs and calls these checks his "pin money," but each deposit, no matter how insignificant, is a reminder to Harvey that being hungry has its rewards.

END NOTES

The Survival Job

Survival jobs, also called bridge jobs, span the gap between careers. Usually temporary, a survival job acts as place holders if, for instance, you need to go back to school or gain additional experience in preparation for a new career. It also helps pay the bills if unemployment compensation is about to run out or bankruptcy is looming. As in Harvey's case, a survival job (or two) may be an imperative.

If you decide to take on a survival job while you are transitioning to a new career, give it some careful thought. Survival jobs have many advantages and could be a strategic next step to building a new career. It also has some downsides.

The Advantages of a Survival Job

In addition to earning a modest income and healthcare benefits, a survival job allowed Harvey to learn new skills and refine old ones. In his job as a fence salesman at Montgomery Ward, he was reminded that he liked interacting with customers, was good at listening and solving problems and enjoyed the challenge of making a sale. He used this survival job to hone his sales skills, bridging them into a new career as a paper goods broker. Ultimately, being successful in a survival job helped restore his self-respect and confidence in his ability to be a contributing member of the workforce. It also helped him clarify his goals and focus on his next career.

The Downside to Survival Jobs

A disadvantage of taking on a survival job while preparing for a new career is that it limits the time you can devote to making a career transition as you put all your energy into making a living wage. As a courier, Harvey often started out early in the morning and worked late into the night to earn enough money to make ends meet. There wasn't enough time in the day to look for more meaningful work, and if he did find himself with time to spare, he was generally too tired to focus on his career.

He also found the courier job demoralizing. His peers were from a much lower socioeconomic strata, the kind of people he had hired and supervised in the meat packing plant and restaurant businesses. Now he was one of them. This was clearly a dead end job and nothing he would ever have considered if he hadn't needed the money. He found he had to leave his pride at home to get through each day.

Harvey also felt demeaned by Paul, his first boss and teacher in the paper products business. But in this case, he could rationalize this assault to his ego by acknowledging that he was getting a useful education that would pay off in the future. He was willing to accept short-term discomfort for long-term gain. He focused his energy on learning as much as he could about the business and not about his relationship with Paul.

How to Make the Most of a Survival Job

If your career transition will take longer than your pocketbook can tolerate, a survival job may give you the time and financial cushion you need to make a well thought out career change. Consider the following:

- Look for survival jobs where you can learn a new skill or enhance a skill that you may need in a future career. For example, if you take on a clerical job, look for opportunities to learn new software and databases. Working in a fast food restaurant can often lead to supervisory experience in the form of training new employees or standing in for your boss when he/she is off site.

- Apply for survival jobs that relate to an interest or hobby. If you love coffee, going to work as a barista may actually be a fun change of pace. If you have an interest in fashion, working retail may give you an opportunity to share your flare for style with less talented clients.

- Be careful not to take on a survival job that will zap your energy. Look for jobs that have weekend and evening shifts and don't require that you bring work home, physically or emotionally. This will free you up to spend the more productive weekday hours pursuing activities to prepare you for your new career like returning to school, participating in an internship or building business connections.

- Make sure your resume is a good fit for the survival jobs you are applying for. If the job requires a high school diploma or some college, you may need to remove your master's degree. The "over qualified" excuse usually means, "We can't afford you." If an employer is looking for someone with 1-3 years of experience, don't advertise that you have fifteen.

- Keep up your spirits. Look for anything positive you can take away from the job. Are you saving gas on a short commute? Making new friends? Giving your day some needed structure? Remind yourself that the survival job is temporary, a place holder in the workforce as you prepare for a new career.

SUGGESTED RESOURCES

Between Opportunities: A Survival Guide for Job Seekers and Career Changers, by Robert Riskin, Aar Dee Aar Publishers Co., 1993

Survival Jobs: 154 Ways to Make Money While Pursuing Your Dreams, by Deborah Jacobson, Broadway, 1998

How to be Happy at Work, by Arlene Hirsch, JIST Works, 2004

How to Survive Your First Job or Any Job: By Hundreds of Happy Employees, by Hundreds of Heads and Ricki Frankel, Hundreds of Heads Books, 2007

Job Savvy, by La Verne L. Ludden, JIST Works, 2008

Career Exploration Inventory, by John Liptak, JIST Works, 2010

CHAPTER II:

John Curley – Creating a Portfolio Career

For 14 years and almost 4,000 shows, John Curley entered the homes of television viewers each weekday evening on one of the Northwest's most popular news programs, KING5 Evening Magazine. Holding the distinction as the longest serving solo host in Northwest history, fans of John Curley were entertained as he bantered with a bevy of celebrities, filmed from exotic locations, performed daredevil feats like the Ironman France, and ran around Seattle performing good deeds in a red mask and cape as The Random Acts of Kindness Man. John loved his job and Evening Magazine viewers loved him. So why change careers?

Tall and slim with frat-boy good looks and a shock of white hair that is incongruous with his young face, John Curley looks like he was destined for a career in television…although it took him 26 years to get there. Diagnosed with dyslexia in the fourth grade, John's academic years were a struggle. Dyslexia is a neurological disorder that makes it difficult to read and write. "But I could talk," said John. "As a child with dyslexia you are either being laughed at or others are laughing with you. I preferred the latter, so I learned to talk and think fast in order to avoid being mocked." John's wit and verbal acumen won over his teachers as well as his classmates as he charmed his way through all twelve grades.

In between numerous attempts at being a college student, John picked up odd jobs. He drove a truck; worked on a chicken farm; dressed in a Mr. Peanut costume and handed out free samples on the street. In 1982, John had accumulated eleven W-2s. He refers to that year as his "building year." He was building a network of contacts. Eventually, through a connection from his father, John landed a job selling medical supplies. His engaging patter and sense of humor were tremendous assets in getting him past the receptionist's desk and into the doctor's office. His income grew as did his confidence, but a restlessness persisted. When John's cousin called to invite him to act in a play he was producing in Scotland, John couldn't resist. A sporadic theater major during his on-again, off-again college years, John was elated at the opportunity to perform in the Edinburgh Theater Festival. In the summer of 1988, John was on a plane headed for Scotland.

In Edinburgh, John became friends with George Takei, the famous actor who is best known for his role as Sulu in Star Trek. One night, George invited John to dinner in one of Edinburgh's most elegant hotel restaurants. Over an exquisitely prepared piece of salmon, John confided his dissatisfaction with medical sales and his sales career in general. "What would you do if you were me, George?" John asked. "I don't give advice," George responded, "but if I *were* you, I would become a T.V. weatherman — everybody loves you, you get to wear nice suits and you don't have to know anything."

George's suggestion may have been tongue-in-cheek, but John took the advice seriously. Living in a pre-Internet world, John headed for the Philadelphia library on his return to the United States. A well-intentioned librarian handed him a book: *How to get into Television,* copyright 1958. That wouldn't do. Next, he was referred to the periodicals on a rack in the corner. On the back of *Broadcast and Cable News* he found this ad: *KJCT Grand Junction, Colorado, seeks outgoing personalities, some knowledge of weather preferred...but not necessary.*

Here was John's big break. He called KJCT and spoke with the station manager, Rick Coran. In fact, he continued to call Coran once a week using every sales technique he had learned until he finally wore the man down. John quit his $130K sales job and headed for Grand Junction to begin his career as a T.V. weatherman that paid $9,600. Good naturedly, he speculates that of the 400 resumes submitted, Coran selected him because he had the most to lose.

On January 12, 1989, John had his first day "on air." He knew it wasn't the best performance he was capable of, but within six months John had perfected his weatherman persona enough to build a decent resume tape and mailed it to stations in larger markets. Over the next three years, his career path looked like a route map in an airline magazine. From Grand Junction, which ranked 185 in the market, John moved to Campaign, Illinois, to Lancaster, Pennsylvania, to Springfield, Virginia. Each move was a stepping stone to advance his career. Eventually he made it to a CBS affiliate in Washington D.C. ranked number nine in the market. For over three years he did the weather and hosted a morning talk show, winning an Emmy along the way. The noted talent agency William Morris took notice and offered John an opportunity to move to Seattle to host *Evening Magazine*. John thought, "Seattle is cool. Everybody drinks coffee and considers it sophisticated to pay $3.00 for a cup of brew." It was 1995. John packed his bags (and favorite coffee mug) and headed for the other coast.

If you're looking for a career that offers some semblance of job security, being a television talk show host is not it. The ratings game is constant and the bottom line is king. For John, the insecurity was like a chronic pain. He would look at the ratings every three months and wonder if he would have a job next week. It also didn't help that the station had been sold to new owners located in Dallas. The stress, however, had a positive effect on John's performance. He honed his craft and kept getting better. He also married, started a family and settled into a comfortable life in the Northwest. Then September 11, 2001 happened, giving John an entirely new career perspective.

"My daughter was born on August 30th, only twelve days before the Twin Towers were attacked. I wanted my new family to be safe. I became very focused on leaving the big city of Seattle and making a small place for ourselves. I said to my wife, Lacey, who was a professional pastry chef, 'We're moving to Vermont and opening a bakery. We'll make donuts. We'll know everyone in town. We'll have kids at our feet and we'll be safe, safe, safe.'"

After consulting a financial advisor and diligently saving, within two years the Curley's were ready to make the move to a small town in Vermont. They even had the wallpaper picked out for the bakery they were going to buy. During the last of his many scouting trips to the east coast before the final move, John had a long conversation with the old woman who owned a B & B across the street. She described what life in a small New England town was really like. She said, "You're going to come here and everyone is going to love you, for about three weeks. After that, the rain will come and the mud season will come, and you'll be making donuts, and you know what? Every day you're going to be throwing them out, because less people will be coming to your bakery. You aren't special any more. Soon your heart will be bitter and you will want to sell the place to some other sucker that comes along with a dream."

John returned to Seattle and told his wife, "I spoke to God. She's got boobs and a thick Vermont accent and we're not doing it." John eventually chose practicality over idealism, but coming to this decision wasn't easy, despite his conversation with the Supreme Being disguised as an old woman from New England.

With dashed dreams, John continued to be successful in his television career. After 11 years as *Evening Magazine* host, the show ranked number one with female audiences 25 to 54 and was considered the number one locally produced show in the country. Apparently the bottom line trumped TV ratings. When it was time to renew John's contract, the new station owners were not willing to negotiate a new contract. To the Texas owners, John Curley was just a line on a piece of paper, and a high priced one at that. John's agent advised, "If you want job security, you'd better get yourself another career."

With less than three years until his contract expired, John tried to remain a cooperative member of the KING5 team. He continued to spend weekends attending community events and emceeing school auctions pro bono. But he was angry and hurt by the fact that he could be so easily replaced.

One Saturday evening while serving as Emcee at the All Saints annual school auction in a small town south of Seattle, John sulked in the corner of the school gymnasium while the auctioneer tried to convince the audience that a hot air balloon ride was exactly what they needed to make their lives complete. "I was thinking, what am I good at? What can I do where I am in control? I thought back to previous jobs and applied the same principles. I am good at talking and cracking jokes. I am good at sales and connecting with people. I am good at being on stage and creating drama. Then I noticed the auctioneer and thought, and I look a hell of a lot better in a tuxedo than he does." Having observed numerous auctioneers over the years, John knew he could do what they did, but better. That night John went home to his wife and announced his new career. "I am going to be an auctioneer."

This time around, John had the Internet to help him with his research. On eBay he found a tape called *Ralph Wade Shows You How to Do It.* Soon he had the *digga-da-digga-da-bigga-da-bagga* auctioneer fast-talk down pat.

Being a celebrity auctioneer is one thing. Being a professional auctioneer is another. Charities were reluctant to hire John because he had no fundraising track record. Once again, relying on his charm and powers of persuasion, John convinced the Seattle Hebrew Academy to hire him for his first professional gig. "When I had ten auctions booked, I began to see my new career taking shape. As I was growing my auction business, the tension I felt at the television station melted away. I saw that I had choices. There was something else I could step into."

Today John owns ten percent of the Northwest market share doing about ninety auctions a year and raising over $1.2 million a month for non-profit organizations. He doesn't consider himself as much an auctioneer as a development director helping organizations to maximize their fundraising potential.

"Henry Ford said 'If you're not learning, you're not living' and I have got to learn and live new things. I am like a storyteller, and I am constantly creating new stories." John also realized that no career is ever truly secure so he has started accumulating careers as well. The auctioneer story is only one chapter of his book. He ran for and was elected to the local City Council. He is also cooking up a television show he plans to pitch to the Discovery Channel. In addition he has created a fundraising business related to charity fun runs and is frequently invited to be a motivational speaker at corporate events. John has created a portfolio of careers which provides him with multiple income streams. He knows his job security doesn't come from a single employer but from within himself. Now he is in control of his career destiny. In a world that sometimes seems out of control, it is a good feeling to have.

END NOTES

Creating the Portfolio Career

In his book, *Job Shift: How to Prosper in a Workplace Without Jobs*, William Bridges predicted that the permanent job is disappearing and all work will eventually be temporary. The full-time or permanent job as we know it is gradually shrinking as a result of new technologies, outsourcing, contract work and most recently a global recession. Today's job security belongs to those individuals who are able to deliver on unmet needs or position themselves as the provider of solutions. If Bridges's predictions are true, then the portfolio career is the path to the future.

A portfolio career is made up of multiple part-time jobs or temporary projects. It could include contract work, freelancing or self-employment in one or multiple professions. Since John's auction business mainly occupies his weekends, he has the flexibility to participate in local politics, work on a television project and engage in other money making ventures to round out his income and his workweek, thus creating a portfolio of careers related to his many interests. Another example of a portfolio career might be an attorney who works a few days a week for a legal practice, teaches a course on contract law at a university and provides consulting services to a handful of corporate clients, using a defined skill set for a variety of related jobs.

The Pros and Cons of a Portfolio Career

The advantage of having a portfolio career is that it offers flexibility, variety, and in many cases a better work/life balance. Some people find that having a portfolio career allows them to participate in their many and diverse interests, like the nurse who has a part-time photography business and bakes gourmet dog biscuits for a local bakery on the side. For most, the portfolio career is appealing in that you are in control of your own fate, not dependant on the whim of an employer for financial security.

On the flip side, portfolio careers require a great deal of self-discipline and superior time management skills as you are often juggling multiple and diverse projects simultaneously. Some portfolio careerists report feeling isolated and anxious regarding the lack of guaranteed income. Networking and marketing are also critical components to keeping your name in the public eye and the jobs coming in, but are not always welcomed tasks, especially with shy types. The reality is most portfolio careers come without healthcare benefits or paid vacation and sick leave, although there are those rare employers who may provide benefits to contractors and part-timers after having worked a certain number of hours.

These are all important factors to think about when considering multiple employment options, especially if you have a low tolerance for risk. A study conducted by exec-appointments.com[1] surveyed executives who left employers to start portfolio careers. At least two-thirds reported they were either "very satisfied" or "satisfied" with their decision. The reasons they listed, beginning with the most rewarding, were the ability to control their own activities, variety, and freedom from corporate politics. The drawbacks included difficulty in finding suitable jobs, financial uncertainty and the high level of networking and self-marketing required.

Things to Consider

If the idea of multiple income streams is appealing to you, here are some helpful tips:

- Identify your skills and interests that are most in demand in industries that are expanding.
- Brainstorm a variety of potential income streams and determine which are most viable. They should vary in their complexity and risk. You want at least one job that isn't too taxing but will bring in steady income.
- Look for every opportunity to build on and expand your network.
- Consider writing articles for publication, blogging or public speaking to create a platform to market yourself.
- Start out slowly. Keep your day job and try moonlighting at first. Gradually expand your projects and options until you feel emotionally and financially ready to say good-bye to traditional employment.

---

1 http://www.quintcareers.com/portfolio_careers.html

SUGGESTED RESOURCES

Jobshift: How to Prosper in a Workplace without Jobs, by William Bridges, Da Capo Press, 1995

Portfolio Life: The New Path to Work, Purpose and Passion after 50, by David Corbett, Kindle Book, Amazon Digital Services, 2006

And what do you do?: 10 Steps to creating a Portfolio Career, by Barrie Hopson & Katie Ledger, A&C Black Publishing, 2010

The Portfolio Career Self-Test, Creative Keys, www.creativekeys.portfoliocareertest.htm

CHAPTER III:

Jeff Levy - The Risky Business of Career Transition

No matter where you are in your stage in life, making a career change is risky business. Jeff Levy has been doing it for most of his career. Not all his risks were successful, but by refining the art of calculated risk-taking, Jeff has learned when to take risks and how much he can afford to lose in order to win in the career game.

Jeff is used to hard work. After all, he has been in the workforce since junior high school. Although he measures no more than 5'7" in height, he is a powerhouse of energy and influence, the kind of man you can't help but look up to.

During his senior year in college, Jeff worked as a manufacturer's rep for a medical supply company while taking classes at night. Although he worked full-time, he managed to graduate in four years with a degree in American History from Fordham University and good intentions to become a teacher, but for economic reasons, he decided to remain in the business world.

Jeff's first big break came about eight years into his career working in a variety of sales positions with medical supply manufacturers. He was recruited by a former boss at Quantro-Control, maker of defibrillators, with an offer to build their New York City territory. Unaware that the management considered this territory the "problem child," Jeff accepted the job because he felt certain that the company was on the brink of cutting edge technology. His hunch was right. Once he figured out how to reach the decision makers, he was able to grow the territory from the bottom 5 percent to the top 10 percent in sales.

"I quickly learned that the only way to get into a hospital was to show up at about 5:30 a.m., before the gatekeepers reported for duty. Once inside, I was able to gain access to the right people, build relationships and make sales."

Jeff hadn't been with Quantro-Control for more than a year when he was faced with another major career decision. The general manager (and a former boss) of a company called Superior Medical invited him to become a regional sales manager. This offer came with a caveat. Jeff would be promoted to general manager of East Coast Operations should the company be acquired by United Hospital Supply, a larger medical supply manufacturer who had been considering such a deal. If the buy-out failed to materialize, however, Superior Medical would close its doors and everyone associated with the company would be out of a job.

Prior to this offer, Jeff had been overlooked for a management position within Quantro. It had been a great disappointment. However, this new proposal was a huge risk on Jeff's part; he had a wife and two small boys to support now. In addition, he was under tremendous pressure from Quantro-Control's top executive who was furious when he found out Jeff was considering such an offer. Jeff knew this move could spring him from sales and catapult him into a management position, the next stop on his career path. Jeff did some research and weighed the risks. If things didn't work out, he could always return to sales. He accepted the offer and after a successful acquisition, he became the general manager of United Dyna Laboratories, a division of United Hospital Supply.

After ten years in the medical supply business, Jeff became disenchanted with the ethics issues surrounding the industry. Were the physicians prescribing his products because they believed in them, or were they hoping to be rewarded with golf outings and exotic trips? When a recruiter approached him with an offer to work in a management position for a company that was manufacturing innovative equipment for executive presentations, Jeff saw his chance to get out of the medical industry and into a business-to-business environment. He accepted the position with this high risk Seattle company, Source Technology, and became manager of the New York office. This time, he gambled and lost. Within a year of joining the company, it declared bankruptcy. Jeff was called to Seattle and given two weeks' notice in addition to the distasteful task of having to fire his employees and close the New York office.

"So now I am in New York without a job. I found that I loved the Northwest and made many excellent business contacts during my visits. Several encouraged me to move to Seattle and help raise the capital to resurrect Source Technology. My wife, Andrea, and I have an adventurous spirit and were willing to take this risk. We sold our house, which provided a financial cushion, packed up our kids and moved to Seattle in 1984."

Jeff spent his first year in Seattle trying to raise capital. Although the rebirth of Source Technology never materialized, he made some impressive connections. "Back in the 1980s, people were more accessible. I met with the senior executives from companies such as Costco, Boeing and Al's Auto Supply. These were people with money looking to make investments and willing to listen to a good story." Aware that opportunities were out there, Jeff partnered with a local investment banker to form Windward Capital. Their business model was to raise money to do leveraged buyouts of small manufacturing companies and then provide the management talent to help them be successful. In 1985, Windward Capital purchased its first small construction company called Spindle Staging, a manufacturer of scaffolding. At the investors' request, Jeff joined the company as Vice President of Marketing, expecting to be there for a year or two to help the company set its course. He eventually became the President and Chief Operating Officer and stayed with the company until 2002, a total of 17 years.

"In the early 1990s we sold Spindle Staging to Erie International. We were now part of a public company and Erie asked me to stay on for a year. It ended up being much longer. I oversaw the growth of Spindle from about $20 million, when we sold it to Erie, to $65 million. By 1997, I was ready to leave. I felt I had done all I could do."

Instead of leaving, however, Jeff discovered that Erie was considering selling its construction division. In a gutsy move, Jeff and a co-worker, Tim Ross, announced that they wanted to buy the division. To the amazement of the Erie Board, Jeff and Tim raised enough capital from the investors they had carefully cultivated to buy Spindle and two other companies that made up the construction division of Erie. They renamed the company Safety Works.

"Tim became the President of Safety Works, managing the finances, insurance and international business. I was the Executive VP and ran all domestic operations. I really thought I had paid my dues and could sit back and relax. This was the last dramatic decision I was going to have to make. Now it was all about doing what I do best and retiring at age sixty or sixty-five with stories to tell my grandchildren." Jeff was forty-eight.

For four more years, Jeff ran a successful operation with 300 employees and seven vice presidents reporting directly to him. He maintained good profit margins and finessed the occasional challenges. Then, one afternoon in 2003, several board members invited Jeff to lunch and announced they had replaced Tim Ross with a GE executive in the hope of giving the company an infusion of new energy. They wanted Jeff to stay, of course, and enticed him with a cash bonus to cover some of Jeff's outstanding financial obligations. Jeff decided to give the new guy a try, but the culture of the company had changed. After several months of trying to adapt to the new CEO's dogmatic management style, Jeff knew he had to leave if he wanted to keep his sanity and integrity intact.

Once again Jeff had to make some serious decisions. He had a wife and son in college and another son in technical school. "My defining moment was to realize that the quality of my life and my relationship with my family and friends meant more to me than a nice paycheck and continued ownership in Safety Work working with a man I couldn't abide. But more significant was the support I got from my wife. She said, 'If you are unhappy, go. If I need to leave school for a while and go to work, so be it. We'll be okay.'"

As he hoped, Jeff was able to negotiate a vacation buy-out, six months' salary and fair value for his ownership in the company. In the summer of 2002, at age fifty-three, Jeff was unemployed. But he was financially and emotionally prepared to take time off to reflect upon what he had learned in his life, what he really liked to do and what he wanted to do next.

"Andrea made me promise I wouldn't look for a job or jump into a new business for at least three months. She bought me a journal and advised me to think introspectively and write down my thoughts."

As Jeff began thinking about his life and his accomplishments, he discovered three things he wanted to avoid: the corporate environment, employees, and bricks and mortar. It was quite a contradiction for a man who had spent thirty years climbing the corporate ladder, overseeing up to 300 employees and managing 70 acres of property. He also made a list of the things he wanted to include in his next career. They included exercise, a social life and the opportunity to mentor others. As he contemplated his criteria he decided to look at franchising and see if there was a franchise opportunity that was a good match. Entrepreneur Source is a franchise that provides consultative and coaching services to other potential franchise owners. It met all of Jeff's criteria.

"I read about Entrepreneur Source in the *New York Times* and liked their methodology of exposing potential business owners to a broad range of franchises. In fact, Entrepreneur Source is a franchise, and I became a client and am now a franchise owner. I went through their process of taking assessments regarding personality, communication style and values. I went through their coaching model and reflected on different kinds of businesses and decided owning an Entrepreneur Source franchise met all of my criteria."

In the last seven years, Jeff has been passionate about working with people who are considering the risk associated with self-employment. He is especially adept at helping his clients to do a calculated risk analysis, determine the downside and the chances for reward, something he had been doing most of his working life. To date he has coached over 92 individuals who have become franchisees. Additionally, he is invited to speak at international conferences and workshops, sits on advisory boards and is frequently recognized for his community involvement and pro bono work. Best of all, he is an active member of The Bellevue Club, his faux office, where he spends equal time building a healthy body and nurturing relationships with friends, business contacts and clients. "People don't find themselves; they create themselves. For me, becoming a Franchise Coach was painfully hard work, but once I had the vision, the risk was definitely worth the reward."

END NOTES

The Art of Risk Taking

Do you have to be a risk taker to be a successful career changer? The answer is yes, but to varying degrees. Risk implies taking action when the outcome is unknown. For many, the word has a negative connotation and is associated with losing. For example, playing the lottery is a blind risk in which you have no control. The potential for a positive outcome is very limited. But taking a calculated risk can also increase your chances for success as Jeff repeatedly proved. How do you distinguish a good risk from the bad?

A Calculated Risk is Based on Research and Facts

When Jeff decided to join Quantro-Control, he researched the industry and felt the technology was "really starting to explode." By gathering as much information from industry experts, business and trade journals and from people he trusted, Jeff was prepared to make a career decision based on logic and data, not feelings alone.

Look at the Worst Case Scenario

If you have little to lose, take the risk. If the risk has the potential to ruin you financially, emotionally or physically, reconsider or at least have a back-up plan that you can live with. When Jeff considered leaving Quantro-Control for United Medical, he knew he would either secure a management position or land on the street. He was willing to take the risk because he felt confident enough in his sales ability that he could find a sales job if the acquisition fell through and he was left without a job. Fortunately, he didn't have to rely on his back-up plan.

Managing Failure

Although Jeff was a successful risk taker during most of his career, a few risks did not have positive outcomes. To the risk adverse, Jeff's decision to leave the stability of the medical supply industry to work for a company that folded within two years, or his decision to move to the West Coast without a job prospect, may seem foolhardy. But to a seasoned risk taker like Jeff, these were opportunities to live what he considered a more appealing lifestyle. At that point, Jeff was also used to taking calculated risks and winning the majority of the time. He had enough confidence in his abilities, his contacts and his willingness to do whatever it takes to provide for his family.

In order to make a change in your life, some measure of risk has to happen. Here are some tips to help you determine whether a risk is worth pursuing.

- Make sure you do your homework and evaluate all the angles before taking a risk.
- Never risk more than you can afford to lose or risk a lot if the return is minimal.
- Avoid risks where the odds against you are great and there are too many factors you can't control.
- Have a back-up plan if the worst should happen.
- Learn from your failures; determine what went wrong and how to avoid repeating your mistakes.
- If you have little to lose, take the risk; it is necessary to move forward.

SUGGESTED RESOURCES

Ready, Willing and Terrified: A Coward's Guide to Risk Taking, by Casey Chaney, Mocha Publishing Company, 1991

Right Risk: 10 Powerful Principles for Taking Giant Leaps in Your Life, by Bill Treasurer, Berrett-Koehler Publishers, 2003

Celebrating Failure: The Power of Taking Risks, Making Mistakes and Thinking Big, by Ralph Heath, Career Press, 2009

You Unstuck: Mastering the New Rules of Risk-taking at Work and in Life, by Libby Gill, Traveler's Tales/Solas House, 2009

The Entrepreneur's Source, www.theesource.com/jlevy

CHAPTER IV:

David Sherman – A New Career with Help from Uncle Sam

David Sherman measures his career success by presidents. Prior to the Reagan administration, his custom design jewelry business was flourishing. With Bush Sr. in office, business started to decline, but he could get by. During the Clinton years, business recovered and was on the upswing. Then Bush Jr. was elected to two terms office and David's business was decimated. It was time for a new president and a new career.

David Sherman's eyes light up and sparkle as vividly as Kashmir sapphires when he talks about any type of gemstone. Even as a kid, he would frequently visit his classmate's family jewelry store and admire the gleaming collection. In 1972, while still in high school, he started a fledgling jewelry import business called Dashasa. As much as he loved rocks, it was the textile classes at the University of Washington that captured his interest. He was going to major in International Business with a double minor in textiles. His decision was reinforced when his textile professor encouraged his choice and connected him to a major textile manufacturer in North Carolina. David was offered a well paid position as a textile designer upon graduation and his future path seemed laid out before him.

David never did complete his last semester at the university, nor did he move to North Carolina. It was an uninspiring marketing class and an impatience to start a career that motivated him to drop out of school and travel to the Far East on a buying trip. He arrived planning to buy fabric and clothing. Interestingly, all the suppliers for textile kept telling him his persona was perfect for jewelry sales and they helped him make those contacts. At first he sold costume jewelry and as his expertise developed, he learned more and more about fine jewelry. He moved Dashasa, out of his bedroom and into a custom jewelry design studio in the Fourth and Pike Building in downtown Seattle. As David's business prospered his showroom space became more elegant and his inventory expanded. He aspired for the most unique pieces available locally.

During the Clinton years, David took a financial risk and invested heavily in a new computer-aided design (CAD) system. The idea was to design jewelry on a computer with the client's input. The concept was customer friendly and also inspired a tremendous inventory of one-of-a kind pieces. At one point, Dashasa boasted the largest color stone collection in the city.

By 2000, David noticed a change in his customers' spending patterns. People were losing jobs and spending less on luxury items, particularly jewelry. He tightened up on his overhead and was borrowing money more frequently to pay the bills. By Bush's second term in office, he realized he was digging himself deeper into debt and was not going to recover. After 32 years in business, he negotiated the closure of Dashasa and began looking for a job. David had just turned fifty.

Fairly quickly, David was hired by a national jewelry company. He started out in sales with the expectation that he would move to the design team. It never happened and David moved on to another national jewelry chain. This chain soon went bankrupt and for the third time in as many years, David was unemployed.

It was 2008 and the unemployment rate was beginning to reach double digits. The jewelry industry was abysmal and his connections were unable to help him out.

David was now collecting unemployment compensation while looking for a job in his industry, even out of state. He was relegated to housekeeper, dog walker, car pool driver and family chef. His morale couldn't have been lower as his savings dwindled and his unemployment benefits were close to ending.

"I kept asking myself, what can I do that will be recession proof? And as I watched my family relish the dinner I had just prepared, I thought, people have to eat. That's when I got the idea to explore culinary school."

He was good with his hands, creative in the kitchen and got great pleasure watching his family enjoy his experiments with cuisine. David's family was enthusiastic about the idea.

By the time David made his decision to enroll in the culinary arts program at a South Seattle Community College, the program was full for the fall semester and he was put on the waiting list for January enrollment. In the meantime, he continued to look for work that paid a living wage and to explore financial aid. He discovered that because there were no jobs in his original field of work, he might be eligible for one of the State's worker retraining programs and could extend his unemployment while he was in training. He applied for this extension but it wasn't approved. Apparently, he wasn't far enough in debt to qualify. He was on his own for tuition for his first semester of culinary school.

By Spring 2009, disaster hit the Sherman household for a second time. David's wife, Cindy, was laid off from her accounting job. As scary as this situation was, it was also David's entry into the world of government aid programs. When David explained his situation to the culinary school coordinator, she sent him to see Jimmy, an advisor in the financial aid office. If David qualified, he would become eligible for other financial aid programs including programs that would subsidize his tuition. Jimmy sent David to the welfare office to apply for food stamps as one of his first steps. Once on welfare, he now qualified for financial aid programs that would assist him on his new career path.

After the welfare office, Jimmy sent David to a WorkSource Center, Washington state's one-stop-shop for employment services. There he met an employment counselor named Stefan. Stefan qualified David for the Unemployment Retraining Program for Professionals, a program created by the Obama administration, which provides individuals with up to $5,000 for retraining. Stefan was also instrumental in helping David find additional grant money for special equipment he needed to buy for specific classes such as a set of commercial knives. With financial help from the government, David was able to complete the two year culinary program within 18 months consistently earning well above the 3.0 grade average required to maintain financial aid. He graduated from culinary school in June 2010.

In March of 2009, during his last semester, David attended a school-sponsored career fair to meet potential employers. He was particularly impressed with the people from a popular local casino and submitted his application on-line as he was instructed by the recruiters. Then he waited by the phone. Nothing happened as is the case with most resumes submitted on-line. When David, discovered a former classmate had been hired at the casino, he approached him with his resume and asked his friend to pass it along. The Sous Chef was impressed and contacted the Human Resources staff. David was invited in for an interview, and hired shortly after.

The casino is a good match for David. They allow him the flexibility to experiment with recipes, spices and color combinations. It nurtures his creativity, not unlike the jewelry business. Recently, a Mystery Shopper came through David's line and he was called out for his exceptional customer service. He hopes this will impact his next review and move him closer to his goal of someday working in catering management. He feels hopeful that during the Obama administration, he will have that chance.

END NOTES

Tips for Funding Your New Career

The good news is that there are a lot of resources available for people who need financial assistance to fund their educational pursuits. The bad news is that they can be hard to find, narrow in scope and sometimes frustrating to negotiate. For example, David was awarded a scholarship from his community college, but it applied for tuition only. Since his tuition was already covered by a Federal grant, he needed the money to pay for books and equipment, but was denied the grant for that purpose and he could not convince them otherwise.

The best place to find out about funding sources for worker retaining is through your state's One-Stop Career Center. You can find the one near you by going to the U.S. Department of Labor or www.careeronestop.org.

These Centers were established in 1998 as a result of the Workforce Investment Act (WIA). They provide a comprehensive range of workforce development activities powered by state and local resources. Some of the programs offered include:

WIA Adult Programs: Serving low income and welfare recipients and some veterans. Services include skills assessment, labor market information, job search and job placement assistance.

Dislocated Worker Program: Serving laid-off workers, workers whose employer has moved or closed down, dislocated homemakers and those who are self-employed but can't work due to economic conditions. This program provides employment and training services.

Senior Community Service Employment Program (SCSEP): Provides job training services for the low income persons 55 years and older.

AARP Worksearch (American Association for Retired Persons): offers worker retraining and employment services to workers over 50 years of age (www.arpworksearch.org)

In addition to government assistance, there are many private sources of financial aid. Depending on your industry, employers and professional or trade associations may offer grants to encourage a fresh crop of workers into their field. David discovered, belatedly, that the National Restaurant Foundation offered grants for continuing education. Private foundations, civic groups and community organizations are sources to investigate for scholarships and grants. Just remember to read the fine print so you understand the nature of any "strings attached."

SUGGESTED RESOURCES

Scholarships for Re-entry Students: Grants and Retraining Assistance for Adults Returning to College, WD Communications, LLC, 1998-2007

501 Ways for Adult Students to pay for college: Going Back to School without Going Broke, by Gen and Kelly Tenabe and Terry Smith, Super College, 2004

The Ultimate Scholarship Book 2010: Billions of Dollars in Scholarships, Grants and Prizes, by Gen & Kelly Tenabe, Super College, 2009

U.S. Government Grants, www.us-government-grants.net

SECTION II: NEEDING TO LEAVE

The Wake Up Call-Leaving for Family or Health Reasons

A routine visit to the doctor can quickly morph into a life-changing event when one's health or the well-being of a family member is at stake. It is also a major catalyst for career change. Marilyn Richards, Robert Eich, Peter Meeker and Larissa Goldin each saw their wake up call as a positive sign for change.

Marilyn embraced her role as Supermom, growing her advertising agency and taking care of her family, until she was diagnosed with Stage 4 Non-Hodgkin's lymphoma and was forced to face her mortality and consider her priorities.

Robert Eich found that the challenges of raising a child with special needs also meant re-evaluating his career choice.

Peter's desire to win his dad's approval grew into a stellar career with NASA, but he had no emotional or spiritual connection with his work. It was beginning to take a toll on his soul. Something had to change and it ended up being his career.

Though successful, Larissa's career in computers took a toll both emotionally and physically. In her search to find ways to improve her health and lessen the stress in her life, she discovered a new dream and the techniques to help her make it a reality.

Chapter V:

Marilyn Richards — Focusing on Positive Choices

Marilyn's career transition evolved through her personal experience as a two-time survivor of non-Hodgkin's lymphoma and her determination to turn a nightmarish experience into a joyous life.

Marilyn Richard's slight, pixie-like appearance is deceiving. She possesses the kind of positive energy that can move mountains and part seas. Married to her college sweetheart in the early '70s, Marilyn and her husband had successful careers in advertising. A series of career moves took them to Los Angeles and then Chicago, where the marriage soured. Marilyn returned to her hometown of Seattle alone, certain she would find employment. Soon after her move, she joined the local office of an international ad agency as VP of Client Services. Her career was on the upswing, and so was her love life. Not long after returning to Seattle, Marilyn renewed an old friendship with Peter Richards, the principal of a small advertising boutique. They fell in love and within the year, they were married.

The advertising business is a volatile industry, constantly expanding and contracting at the whim of its clients. Eight months into her marriage, Marilyn's employer decided to close its Seattle office and move the business to Los Angeles. Facing the prospect of unemployment, Marilyn and her boss, Jim McFarland, debated the merits of opening their own boutique, full-service agency. They were confident they would be able to recruit enough clients and, in the mid-1990s, the economy could easily support another creative shop. McFarland and Richards opened their doors in Seattle's historic Pioneer Square. Soon after, they merged their business with Marilyn's husband and his partner, Gary Graf, to form McFarland, Richards and Graf.

As their business expanded, so did the Richards' family. Marilyn and Peter had two sons and the agency had grown to eleven employees. Marilyn finally had the working mom's life she dreamed of, but she hadn't anticipated the consequences. "It was so hard to be the mom of these two little kids, manage a household and then try to be a principal in a marketing firm with three male partners. There were days that I could hardly breathe." As the clients became more demanding and there were more employees to deal with, Marilyn felt her enthusiasm for the advertising business increasingly challenged.

In the fall of 2003, as she was approaching her forty-sixth birthday, Marilyn felt a small lump on her collarbone but was too busy to think much of it. Although family members had died from various cancers, including her mother at the age of forty-six, she was sure the odds were in her favor. After all, she ate right and lived a healthy, spiritual lifestyle. She was convinced there would be no cancer in her life.

Positive thinking was not enough to keep the tiny knot on her collarbone from growing into a giant lump on her neck. "The biopsy came back and it was, in fact, stage four non-Hodgkin's lymphoma. I was unbelievably shocked. The doctors wanted to begin chemotherapy right away."

After a day of processing, the idea of having cancer still seemed unreal. Calmly, Marilyn called her partners together to discuss a leave of absence. "I temporarily gave all my assignments to my loving business partners. They kindly and generously accepted my work, and I just walked away. Suddenly, the crushing responsibility of being a successful businesswoman had disappeared."

The new challenge Marilyn faced was six rounds of extremely toxic chemotherapy treatments. Harder still was telling her children, family and friends about her illness. Soon after her disclosure, the lasagna and tuna casseroles started appearing at her front door, brought by well-meaning parents from her boys' school and members of her church. In between the overwhelming outpouring of concern, there were tears and hair loss. Marilyn struggled with the question, "Why me?" She was a good mother, went to church regularly and practiced a healthy lifestyle. Weren't these antidotes powerful enough to keep cancer away?

One afternoon, after an especially difficult, bone weary day, Marilyn got a call from her priest, requesting a visit. She thought he would come and say 'bless you,' mumble a nice prayer and leave. But that didn't happen. After accepting an offer of herbal tea and engaging in the requisite small talk, the young Jesuit looked directly at Marilyn and said in a matter-of-fact tone, "This is your path. You must walk it. Jesus didn't like his path either and neither did the Saints." He finished his tea and left.

This advice infuriated Marilyn. She refused to accept her cancer as her fate. As she sat for eight hours in the chemo chair, she had a lot of time to reflect. The priest's words filled her mind as the chemo cocktail filled her body. Perhaps she was at a fork in the road and this was an opportunity to choose a new path. During the next twenty-four rounds of treatment while her fellow chemo patients dozed, read or watched the daily soaps, Marilyn gained an overwhelming desire to take control. She devoured books on her illness, wrote her thoughts and feelings in a journal and evaluated the truths in her life.

During the next few months she faced her own mortality head on. She allowed herself to mourn the loved ones she had lost to cancer in the past and to exam her own feelings about death. At some point she was able to reconcile both, and her sense of dread turned into a feeling of empowerment. She made a decision not to be a victim to cancer, but rather to create the type of life that would bring her joy. "My diagnosis is cancer. I have no hair. I'm twenty pounds lighter and people would say, 'You look so happy. You're glowing.'"

Marilyn's positive reformation had a magnetic effect on others. First the PTA president called her to ask if she would talk to a mother of twins who had breast cancer. Over time, more women with cancer began to seek Marilyn out. She would meet them on Tuesdays and Thursdays, her days off from the ad agency, at a local coffee shop. She would help them answer difficult questions, from the obvious to the sublime — "Which naturopath do you recommend?"; "How should I tell my husband and children?"; "Why do I feel like I am being punished?"; "Where is God in all this?" Marilyn noticed she was energized and full of life on these days. The rest of the work week had the opposite effect.

One day she received a call from a client who manufactured health and wellness products. He was upset that the vivacious blond on the new marketing brochure was not blond enough.

"He was complaining to me about hair color and I am thinking about the women I have been working with who have no hair at all, who don't know if they will live long enough to see their hair grow back. It was the ultimate irony."

Shortly after this incident, another small knot appeared near Marilyn's collarbone. Because of its proximity to her artery, the doctors decided against a biopsy. Without a biopsy, there could be no treatment. "Lymphoma can come and go like crabgrass," the doctor tried to reassure her. "You look great. You feel great. Go home and we will see you in a couple of months."

Marilyn was astounded, realizing that she couldn't count on her doctors for help. Feeling shocked and abandoned, she reminded herself that she alone was responsible for her recovery. She had explored and pondered her life with cancer and exhausted all there was to read and study. She began restructuring her life and took control of her healing. Through deep spiritual work and meditation she identified the things in her life that brought her happiness and discarded the negative influences that created stress and lowered her spirits. She learned to say "no" to the activities and people that drained her energy and focused on the things that brought her joy. It was clear that the energy-depleting advertising business had to go. Helping other women face cancer was what energized her and brought her immense happiness. So Marilyn set out to create for herself what she refers to as an extraordinary life. In the spring of 2007, she said a final good-bye to her partners at McFarland, Richards and Graf and embarked on her new career, coaching women with cancer.

Marilyn's career as a healing coach is evolving. She still regularly meets with cancer survivors at the local coffee shop, although now she is a registered counselor and coach offering support and resources to cancer patients and others dealing with trauma in their lives. Frequently, she is invited to conduct workshops and deliver motivational speeches at conferences, church retreats and association meetings. Most people find their way to Marilyn through the "mommy grapevine," as she puts it. Her clientele is also changing. Although most of the people who come to her have cancer, she sees many businesswomen and men who are experiencing marital troubles, problems at work, the death of a loved one or other traumas in their lives.

"A zest for life really mobilizes the immune system to fight back against cancer. That is really the essence of my story. I found what I love to do. I found my calling. Although, I should say, it found me. It was already there. I just didn't know it."

END NOTES

Victim or Victor — You Choose

It is easy to become a victim to cancer, or any disease for that matter. We become submissive to doctors, medical procedures, a host of medications and the concern of family members and friends. When Marilyn's cancer reoccurred and the doctors refused treatment, she had two choices. She could have surrendered to anger, depression and self-pity, or she could take control and reconstruct a life that gave her joy. She chose the latter and set out to create what she described as an extraordinary life.

As in illness, people can also feel victimized by their work. They become subservient to their bosses, a paycheck, a lagging job market or their family's expectations. They feel trapped in their jobs and helpless, too paralyzed or resigned to take action. But they have choices, too. They can choose to go to work everyday and be miserable, or they can take control and create a course for positive change.

Marilyn already had in her possession several tools to help her create her extraordinary life. She was a positive person by nature, but she also had great self-awareness through the work she put into journaling, reading, mediation and therapy. She was able to identify and eliminate the negative forces in her life and surround herself with the positive. Her focus was on being with family, friends and people in her professional network that provided love and encouragement. She also focused on positive thoughts and activities. She gave herself permission to say "no" to the pressures and people she did not want in her life.

Embrace the Positive

Norman Vincent Peal, the father of the "positive thinking" theory said, "If you have zest and enthusiasm, you will attract zest and enthusiasm." He believed that by banishing the negative from your life, improvement would follow. He wrote, "Your unconscious mind ... [has a] power that turns wishes into realities when the wishes are strong enough."[2]

Studies and anecdotal evidence repeatedly prove Peal's theory that positive thinking improves health, relationships and life in general. If you are considering a career change, having a positive attitude is imperative to a successful transition. Avoid negative thoughts which create self-doubt, inertia and excuse-making behaviors that aren't conducive to moving forward. Stay away from friends and relatives who may be scared or envious of your plans for change and try to sabotage you with hurtful comments or criticism. By engaging in positive thinking, participating in motivational and healthy activities and creating a supportive network, career changers find they have the ability to make extraordinary changes in their lives.

There are many resources available to develop positive thinking including books, CDs, DVDs, websites, workshops and lifestyle coaches. They offer exercises and techniques such as journaling, visualization, affirmation and meditation. They are filled with inspiring stories of people who have changed their lives in joyful ways, by embracing positive thinking.

---

2 http://normanvincentpeale.www.hubs.com

SUGGESTED RESOURCES

You Can If You Think You Can, by Norman Vincent Peal, Fireside, 1987

Positive Imaging: The Powerful Way to Change Your Life, by Norman Vincent Peal, Ballantine Books, 1996

Take Time for Your Life, by Cheryl Richardson, Broadway, 1999

The Power of Positive Thinking, by Norman Vincent Peal, Fireside Edition Revised, 2003

Everyday Positive Thinking, by Louise Hay and Friends, Hay House 2004

Success through a Positive Mental Attitude, by Napoleon Hill and W. Stone, Pocket, 2007

Change Your Mind and Your Life Will Follow, by Karen Casey, Conari Press, 2008

Transformational Coaching & Consulting, www.marilynrichards.com

CHAPTER VI:

Robert Eich - Turning Life Lessons into a Career

Raising a child is difficult at best. Raising a special needs child is an even greater challenge. With considerable fortitude, Robert Eich learned how to navigate a complex system of educational, medical and social services for his special needs daughter, resulting in some unexpected outcomes for his career.

Robert Eich's intense curiosity fuels his love of learning. After graduating from a large Midwestern university in 1976, he studied German History at Columbia University, receiving his PhD in 1985. He went on to teach at Dalhousie University in Halifax, Nova Scotia, for a year and also began publishing a series of articles, all peer-reviewed, on German social history. Shortly before receiving his doctorate, Robert met his future wife, Clara, a first-year internal medicine resident at a large hospital in New York City. They developed a strong relationship that survived Robert's trips between Halifax and New York.

The itinerant life of a young academic had little appeal after Clara was offered the chance to pursue full-time AIDS research at the University of California in San Francisco. Robert moved west with little hesitation. The two married in 1988 and settled into a bright flat just two blocks from Golden Gate Park.

"This meant a fresh start," said Robert. "To maintain my interest in history, I developed a friendship with Lorrie Olson through an organization of independent historians to which we both belonged." Lorrie helped Robert ease into a new career by hiring him to work with her technical writing group at Bank of America. For two years, he was one of four writers responsible for developing policy and procedure manuals for Bank of America's California branches. Subsequently, and for another two years, he documented trading systems for the bank's capital markets Research & Development group.

In addition to his day job, Robert joined a thirty-something entrepreneur and full-time writer in a small start-up company called Petroglyph. There he contributed to the development and marketing of the company's Editorial Adviser software, a comprehensive HyperCard guide to English grammar and usage for the Macintosh. (HyperCard was a Macintosh-based precursor of the Web's hypertext language.) After this experience, Robert began copy-editing computer books part-time for Ziff-Davis Press. Loving the book business, he left Bank of America in 1992 to become a product manager at Sybex, the oldest publisher of computer books and now an imprint of Wiley. In 1994, filling in for an author, Robert wrote a computer book for Sybex called *Access to the Internet*. The book was a success and launched Robert on a ten-year career as author of seven computer-related books, including *AOL's Student's Guide to the Internet* and *Wiley's 100 Tips & Tricks for Excel*. Life, however, was about to take Robert in another direction, literally and figuratively.

Robert and Clara had two children in the early 1990s, a boy and girl, who were both born premature after difficult pregnancies. With Robert's encouragement and assistance with raising the children, Clara managed to finish her research at UCSF. In 1994, a newly-minted PhD, she was offered a research position in Bethesda, Maryland.

"I was eager to move back east in order to be closer to my parents. I also wanted to live in an area with strong communities, four seasons and good schools, which was now an important consideration." He was able to continue his career in technical publishing by joining the staff at a publishing service that catered to government, legal and business professionals. There he was responsible for one of the first guides to the Internet for business users. Within a year, drawn to the dynamic world of Internet business in the DC area, he joined America Online as the manager of Internet-related online content. Continuing his activity in computer books, he also wrote *AOL's Official Guide to the Internet*, revising it through six editions.

As his kids became the focus of his life, Robert found himself drawn back into the world of learning and teaching. While his son was developing normally, it quickly became clear that his daughter, Leah, was missing milestones such as sitting up and using simple language. Instead, she displayed a number of physical, language, and social differences. Several doctors had placed her on the autism spectrum, though Robert and Clara quickly found that such categories can have limited value in the day-to-day work of raising a unique child with her own developmental path.

As Robert took Leah on the weekly rounds of speech and occupational therapy, daughter and father both learned the art of play therapy from a developmental psychologist. "By observing their interactions, I acquired a strong intellectual and personal interest in the lives and educational realities of 'atypical children' like Leah." For his family, the "atypical" became the norm, which made life challenging...and fun. These experiences inspired Robert to take a new direction in his career.

With a renewed and very personal interest in education theory, Robert began to seek a path back to the world of history and learning without giving up the skill sets he had acquired over the previous decade. Building on his technology background, he enrolled in the educational technology leadership program at a local university, with a specialty in assistive technology for children with special needs. In addition to a master's degree, he also pursued a teaching certificate in both special education and history.

Since 2003, Robert has had the chance to combine his life-long love of history with his more recently-acquired skills in technology as a teacher in a special-needs high schools in the Washington area. Serving as a full-time teacher of world history, US history and economics, and a part-time tutor of students with learning difficulties, he has created a rewarding niche for himself in his community. He continually learns across several areas of interest and enjoys watching his students—and children—grow, learn and succeed.

"Being in special education feels like home. I can't imagine being in any other field. It is a wonderful opportunity to work with such unique children and their families and to feel I'm making a difference while doing what I love."

END NOTES

Finding Role Models

Role models can have a powerful influence on one's career choice. Just ask a child. When my nephew was young, he needed extensive dental work. For years he talked about becoming an orthodontist, until he saw a David Lynch movie and was convinced he wanted a career as a film maker. That was until he heard Dick Dale's, "Miserlou" soundtrack on *Pulp Fiction* and decided to write musical scores.

Role models are everywhere — in the media, books, movies, and of course, the people we interact with in real life. Reading about or observing how others have become successful, particularly if they've had to overcome great obstacles or share core values, can inspire and motivate others to action. Robert Eich wasn't actively looking for role models, and he wasn't consciously considering changing careers, but through his intellectual curiosity, academic studies and observing the professionals who supported his daughter's physical, academic and social growth, he was inspired to parlay his strengths and interests into a new career.

If you are considering a career change, your sensitivity to the success of others in their occupations is already heightened. The next step is to begin your research.

Information Meetings

Identify the person or people of professions that interest you and arrange for an information meeting to talk about what they do. It is best to approach them through a mutual friend or acquaintance if you can find one. Otherwise, write a compelling letter or e-mail requesting a meeting to learn more about the individual's occupation and how they got where they are today. Ask for a half-hour meeting and stick to your timeframe. People enjoy talking about their professional achievements, but going over your thirty-minute time request may be taking advantage of their generous nature. Be prepared with lots of questions that will help you get enough information to determine if this occupation is both a realistic goal and a good fit for you. Some questions you might want to consider include:

- How did you decide to become a teacher/dentist/actuarial?
- What was your educational background or training?
- Describe your career progression.

- What do you like most/least about your work?
- What type of skills and personal traits are required to be successful in this occupation?
- How much money can someone expect to make entry/mid/senior-level?

Job Shadowing

Job shadowing has become such a popular concept that a special day has even been named for it: National Job Shadow Day. Usually falling on Groundhogs Day, this day is an opportunity for employers to invite students into their companies to follow a professional at work. The idea is to provide future job seekers with an inside look at what people do minute-by-minute on the job so that they will be better prepared to select a career in the future.

Although shadowing is usually reserved for students, the audience most likely to benefit from a job shadowing experience is adults considering a career change. Unfortunately, most career changers don't think of job shadowing as a research tool for exploring new careers.

Career changers often return to school or give up well-paying jobs to accept entry level employment only to find their new profession isn't what they expected. Before committing the time, money and emotional energy required to change careers, include job shadowing in your career exploration tool kit.

SUGGESTED RESOURCES

Exploring the World of Work Through Job Shadowing, by Susan Reese, Amazon.com, 2005

Role Models: Examples of Character and Leadership, by Joseph M. Hoedel, Character Development Group, Inc., 2005

Models of Human Occupations, Gary Kielhofner, Lippencott, Williams & Wilkins, 2007

Real Role Models: Successful African Americans beyond Pop Culture, Joah Spearman & Louis Harrison, University of Texas Prss, 2010

InternMatch, www.internmatch.com

Chapter VII:

Peter Meeker – Family Influence on Career Choices

Our families have a powerful influence on our career choices. The type of work we do, professional expectations and beliefs about money are determined in the subtle messages we receive from our families as young children. Peter's father had a profound impact on his career choices that lead him down two very different but successful career paths.

Peter Meeker was the youngest of five children born to Swedish immigrants living in South Dakota. Having fled Sweden for "the promised land" just after World War II, Peter's parents arrived with $300 and little knowledge of the language. As most immigrants, they worked hard to establish a comfortable life for their family. Peter's father worked as a baker while his mother raised their five children, all of whom were born within the first seven years of living in the United States. A child of devout Catholics, Peter remembers his father as very demanding and emotionally explosive, while his mother remained distant and emotionally out of reach.

"My dad became a baker at the age of sixteen, but if he had the opportunity he would have chosen a career in electronics. He loved to work on electronics projects. I learned to please him by doing the things he wanted to do, so I spent a lot of time with him in the basement working on his projects. I ended up becoming an electrical engineer, which wasn't a coincidence. I ended up fulfilling my father's dream."

From fourth grade on, Peter worked hard to get straight A's, the only grade acceptable to his father. Like his siblings, the children in the Meeker family were over-achievers. His brothers became doctors and his sisters also went into the medical field. During his senior year of high school, Peter was offered three scholarships. He accepted a full scholarship and attended a school of engineering in the West.

It was during college that Peter experienced the darkest period of his life. He slipped into a deep depression which was eventually diagnosed as bi-polar disorder. It had a crippling effect on his ability to perform in school and created an emotional wedge between him and his parents, who found mental illness hard to understand. After several attempts at college, with periods of hospitalization in between, Peter's condition was finally stabilized through appropriate medications. It had taken him over ten years to complete a Bachelor's and Master's degree in engineering, but by 1986 he was working for a research group that contracted with NASA to develop cutting edge technology.

"I was affiliated with that research group for fifteen years and became an expert in my field. Some of the technology I designed was being used around the world and even ended up going to Mars." During his last five years with the organization, Peter was working on architectures for the next generation in space, working with scientists from around the world.

Although his health remained stable and he was highly regarded in his work, Peter felt a void in his life that he couldn't explain. He had created a spiritual life of his own making after having left the Catholic Church at the age of twenty-two, much to his parent's dismay. He would occasionally take sojourns by himself to get away from work and reflect on life. When his research group was stationed in New Mexico in 1995, he found it to be the perfect place to get away for quiet weekends, explore open spaces and commune with God.

During one such retreat, Peter visited Fort Union, north of Santa Fe. The initial fort, built during the Civil War, was so badly constructed the soldiers were said to have slept outdoors to avoid the bed bugs and crumbling adobe. "I had just finished watching a film in the interpretive center and stepped outside to explore the Fort. The day was glorious, but I was surrounded by ruins. That's when I felt I heard a quiet voice inside me say, "I don't want you to work for things that don't last."

Over the next five years Peter continued to work as an engineer, but he also began connecting with people and looking for more meaning in his life, something that would ignite his heart. He occasionally took time off from his job to do missionary work for a humanitarian organization. Instead of living so much of his life inside his own head as he had in the past, he was gaining more awareness of the world around him. At one point he was asked to lead a church group. He started thinking about becoming a missionary or perhaps pastoring.

One day on his way to work at a plush, new research center, Peter was stopped at a light when a homeless man staggered across the street in front of his car. He had a scraggly black beard, matted hair and wore a slimy-looking khaki coat. As Peter watched the man stumble his way to the underpass, he felt a profound sadness for this human being. For the first time in his life Peter was overcome by a deep feeling of compassion. He was aware that his overly-suppressed emotional psyche was starting to crack. Having grown up in a demanding and bitter environment he had learned to suppress his emotions. He taught himself not to feel. Even though his dad had died several years earlier, Peter had continued to hold his own heart prisoner. It was going to take a lot of emotional work to set it free.

By the end of 2002, Peter moved to the Northwest with his research group. His work was being recognized by members from the international space community and his career was on an upward trajectory. But his heart was opening up to new possibilities. "I had lived in my head all my life like a robot. Now there was this world of emotion I had discovered. It was turbulent, scary and beautiful because I found I could care about people, not just things."

While working as an engineer, Peter began seeing a therapist. Not the kind he had seen in his past that would spent ten minutes checking his blood levels and prescribe some pills, this individual was someone he could really talk to and connect with, someone who helped him explore his feelings. Through therapy he became increasingly interested in matters of the heart and the name of a Graduate School kept coming up in conversations. "I learned that this was a school that would engage more than my head; it would engage my heart. I knew the work would be challenging emotionally, but I was desperate for this connection."

After eight months notice and the well wishes of his co-workers, Peter left the world of space engineering and entered graduate school to become a relationship counselor. He was forty-four. "My mom was against it and my dad, if he had been alive, would have freaked. But I also had them to thank, because the brokenness of my past was the driving force for my future."

An important part of learning to become a therapist is experiencing therapy. Peter found a counselor with whom he formed a profound bond. His heart opened wider and he experienced tenderness and caring. "I was an emotionally disconnected man who had become captivated with relationships and love much later in life. I am a man who now is all about relationships."

Peter has been a counselor for about five years. He uses Relational Psychotherapy, which is based on the study of relationships and early attachments, and Lifespan Integration Therapy, which has its basis in neuroscience and trauma research. Using these therapeutic approaches allows him to tap into his engineering persona because attachment in terms of neuroscience relates to strong relationships. He believes that learning to love yourself and others makes for a more fulfilling life. He also knows from experience that kindness and self-acceptance open space for change.

END NOTES

Family Influence on Career Choice

Through the ages, family has played a significant role in career choice. In the past, family names frequently reflected the father's occupation. If a son was born a Goldsmith, Carpenter, Farmer or Cartwright, he most likely followed in his father's footsteps. The industrial age created more occupational choices as well as opportunities for daughters to enter the workforce. Although the family names and occupational traditions were no longer determining factors in one's career choices, the influence of family expectations, values and beliefs about money and success on an individual's career choice remain profound.

Both of Peter's career choices were influenced by his family. He developed an interest in electronics and became an engineer to gain his father's acceptance, but growing up in a home that lacked acceptance and affection also had a tremendous influence on his psyche as he grew older. Once he discovered that he was capable of deep emotions, something he had not experienced in childhood, he realized there was another side of his personality yet to be discovered. Through therapy, he chose to become a therapist and help others improve relationships. This career choice was in contrast to the lifestyle and values his parents had modeled as he was growing up.

Positives and Negatives of Family Influence

Family influence on one's career choice can be good or bad depending on a number of factors including personality traits, belief systems, motivations, aptitude and economic influences. For example, a young man growing up in a family of teachers may demonstrate the patience, love of learning and creativity to follow the family tradition and find teaching a rewarding career. On the other hand, if his temperament demonstrates keen ambition, strong leadership skills and expectation of financial gain, he may find a career in teaching less than satisfying and be more suited to a role in business or entrepreneurship. It is often difficult to separate family pressure from personal motivation and desire. If they aren't compatible, it is easy to make the wrong career choice.

In Peter's case, neither career was a choice of right or wrong. He enjoyed being an engineer and is thriving in his new career as a relationship therapist. However, his motivation for engaging in his careers was quite different. The former career was selected to gain family approval while his career as a therapist was internally motivated and not driven by his mother's esteem. Peter's career transition was a courageous act of self-discovery and determination to make a change in his life in a way he believed was positive and necessary to self-fulfillment in employment.

Understanding Family Influence on Career Change

Career Counselors have many techniques to help their clients assess family influences and use this information in a positive way, ranging from surveys and questionnaires to career timelines and genograms. The Career-o-gram is one such tool. Similar to a family tree, it focuses on the career history of one's family members and is presented pictorially in order to spot patterns and themes more easily. Being able to assess family influences along with a self-analysis of personal values and individual strengths can provide valuable information and reinforce long-term success when selecting a new career path.

SUGGESTED RESOURCES

Hand-me-down Dreams: How Families Influence Our Career Paths and How We Can Reclaim Them, by Marky H. Jacobson, ThreeRivers Press, 2000

A Family Genogram Workbook, by Israel Galindo, Elaine Boomer, David Reagan,
Educational Consultants, 2006

Family Matters: The Influence of the Family on Career Decision-making, by Robert C. Chope, ProEd, 2006

The Father Factor: How Your Father's Legacy Impacts Your Career, by Stephan Poulter, Prometheus Books, 2006

Chapter VII:

Larissa Goldin — Visualizing a New Career

Larissa Goldin has always been in the business of building businesses for herself and others. It is as if she can gaze into a crystal ball to see a thriving business. Then she steps back and figures out how to make it happen. She calls it "magic wand thinking" and it has been a significant tool in helping her transition from the world of technology to the world of wellness and health and led to the founding of Dreamclinic.

At first glance, Larisa could be taken as everyone's favorite third grade teacher: inquisitive, intelligent, supportive, and expecting the best of everyone. Endowed with a stubborn streak, once she has decided on something, it happens. As an undergraduate she studied mathematics, as her family expected her to play a role in science or economics. The problem was that she found math boring and could not stay awake in class. One day, she met a classmate with a bunch of books under her arms.

"I'd read most those books, and I wished out loud that I could get credit for that. My friend said, 'Why don't you?' It was a 'Why Not' moment. So I literally got up off the grass—I was sitting on the grass on campus—and I walked to the English department and switched my major to English. That was a great decision and I really enjoyed it. It turns out that I have a knack for communication."

This would not be the last time that Larisa would find and pursue her own path regardless of others' expectations. After completing college in the late 1980s, Larissa worked for a company that exported computer supplies. When she offered to help the owner expand his business in the U.S., he gave her the green light. With a lot of cold calling, she built the company's U.S. sales and helped the business grow from two to ten employees. She learned a lot about computer products and the export business, but as far as professional development was concerned, the company didn't offer her a future. The owner didn't believe women were tough enough to be managers. Larissa couldn't abide this kind of thinking and needed to prove him wrong. She quit and started her own business, Zelcor, selling similar computer products. Without poaching her former employer's clients, using the Yellow Pages and America On-line as her weapons, she built her business to four employees and $1.2 million in sales. She was only in her mid-twenties.

While an owner of Zelcor, Larissa became very comfortable with technology. She maintained a network of computers and printers. She taught herself database development and implemented a system to manage inventory and customer information. Because Larissa put a lot of effort into the database to make it nimble and tailored for her company, it became a significant business asset.

Larissa was financially successful. She had proved her former boss wrong. Running a company had increased her confidence that she could handle new situations, but something was wrong. Larissa was miserable.

"My parents were very conservative and success was measured financially. I accepted that. I didn't necessarily have a passion for computer supplies. It just happened that I quickly learned the industry and was good at sales. It was the financial success that was driving me at that time. When I experienced health issues, it really made me reevaluate a lot of the things. Just because I had employees and money, it did not provide enough motivation or joy for me to keep going."

After three years of working fourteen-hour days, the physical manifestation of stress was ruining her life. She was in constant pain that was affecting her work and her relationships. The triggering event occurred one day when she became enraged at an employee who had asked a simple question. At that moment, she caught herself and recognized that this was a problem that she had to fix. Her declining health motivated her to sell the business and take time to re-evaluate her priorities.

"When I sold my company, it was a dark time for me because I felt I had failed. Suddenly, I no longer held the title of President. But without the tremendous pressures I had the chance to restore my health and visualize a truly fulfilling life for myself. I began to see everything as an opportunity."

Determined to improve all aspects of her health, she got massages and learned yoga and meditation. She started paying attention to the labels on the foods she was eating and educated herself about nutrition and preventative health. Reading books by Anthony Robbins, Deepak Chopra, Marianne Williamson, and Shakti Gawain helped her recognize and remove the filters and limits in her beliefs and enabled her to visualize the kind of life she wanted to live.

Waving her "magic wand," Larisa imagined a world in which there were no obstacles. She pictured what a truly fulfilling life would look like, and then what would be necessary to achieve that life. Based in her belief that all people deserve good health and well-being, she envisioned a place for yoga classes, massage, meditation, lectures, and wellness classes. She hadn't found a venue quite like it. It came alive in her mind's eye as she designed the facility, chose the colors, and selected the furniture. Ten years later, this vision became Dreamclinic.

Nine months after selling her company, Larissa was ready to return to work. Unwilling to put herself in a box and limit her possibilities, she looked at jobs in sales, software training, education, and writing. Her goal was to find a position where she could learn how others ran successful businesses. It was 1995 and the world wide web was about to explode. She was familiar with the member's forums on AOL and realized that the internet would be much bigger and would provide many opportunities for interesting work and growth. She accepted a job at InstallShield as a Webmaster, which was a new occupation at that time. InstallShield provided installation development tools for software products.

This was a fantastic opportunity. Not only did she learn about the software applications that were using InstallShield, she also learned how to create and maintain web sites. After building an award-winning site for InstallShield, Larissa was recruited to the development team to lead the building of InstallShield's first web based product, *Install-FromTheWeb*. It allowed users to install software just by clicking a button on a web page.

In 1999, Larissa moved to Seattle to join a company started by a friend, 4thpass, which developed Java based software for the telecommunications industry. While she continued to work in high tech, she also was preparing to make her dream a reality. She took classes in the evening to become a massage therapist. She applied to the Executive MBA program at the University of Washington to complete the business skills that she had previously developed when she ran her first company.

In 2002, 4thpass was purchased by Motorola. Larissa's job was redundant and she was laid off. Larisa's plan had been to continue to work developing software as she established Dreamclinic; however, reflecting on the opportunity the layoff provided, she said "Why not?" As a means to reduce risk and to gauge the market, Larissa set up a massage studio in her house. Within months she outgrew that and rented a room from a running coach. A year later there was enough business to rent a building. Today, Dreamclinic has forty full time and part time credentialed massage therapists on the payroll.

Opportunities found their way to the Dreamclinic. Word of mouth from satisfied customers led *Seattle Magazine* to review the facility. Several major employers in Seattle requested services at their work sites. Client services expanded as did class offerings. In addition to massage, Dreamclinic began offering acupuncture, yoga, meditation and a series of evening seminars with titles such as *The Empowerment Dynamic* and *Explore Consciousness.*

Of course, it didn't hurt that she was also able to apply her knowledge of technology. By using search engine optimization techniques, Larissa was able to ensure that Dreamclinic appeared on the first page of major search engines such as Google, Yahoo and MSN, making it easy for potential clients looking for massage to find Dreamclinic on the internet. In order to insure that she had sufficient staff, she used her computer skills to establish findtouch.com, an online contingent staffing market place for the Health and Beauty sector.

"Have a clear vision with specific intent; have faith and the opportunities will come," Larissa says.

Her magic wand thinking continues as she visualizes a second Dreamclinic opening in Seattle and eventually a chain of Dreamclinics sprouting up across the country. Is she headed for another burn out?

"I now know when to take a day off. I give myself a lot of slack. I promised myself that I would run Dreamclinic in a way that is all about a healthy lifestyle. My health will not come second to the business. After all, as Dreamclinic promotes health, I need to ensure that I preserve my own. I have to be true to my beliefs."

END NOTES

Tips on the Art of Visualization

Athletes commonly use visualization techniques to enhance their performance. In the sixth game of the 1975 World Series, Dwight Evans who was the right fielder for the Boston Red Sox visualized going into the stands to catch a ball. Sure enough, Joe Morgan with the Cincinnati Reds hit a ball which would have been a home run except that Evans caught it as it was going into the stands. Visualization is the ability to create one's own reality within the mind. It is more than thinking about what you want. It is envisioning life as a reality. As hockey player Wayne Gretsky put it, "I skate to where the puck is going to be…"

Many students of visualization believe it is more than simply creating a picture in the mind. It involves visualizing all the senses—hearing, smelling, feeling— as well as experiencing the emotions. Larissa had designed the Dreamclinic in her mind in great detail before ever putting her vision on to paper. Once she was completely aware of her vision, she became more observant to opportunities. This is called 'conscious attraction.' As her vision became reality, she began to attract opportunities subconsciously. In other words, possibilities came to her because her vision was so ingrained. This is called 'subconscious visualization.'

Visualization Techniques

Visualize in the first person: Don't allow yourself to be on the outside looking in on the action. Picture yourself involved in your dream, actually doing the activity and making it happen. If your vision is becoming a teacher, don't watch yourself in front of the classroom. Actually jump into your vision and do the teaching.

Use all your senses: Add color to your vision. Include music and fragrance. Animate your vision as if it were happening in 3-D or on an IMAX screen. Add as much detail as you possibly can. Feel the joy of students getting excited about learning. Experience the exhilaration when that light bulb goes on for a struggling child…and you were the reason for it happening.

Create a visual: Cut pictures from magazines to create a collage on poster board or draw images of your vision in crayon or paint. Shrink your artwork down and laminate it so you can carry your vision around and refer to it during the day.

Spend time with your vision: Find a quiet spot and devote 10 to 30 minutes each day visualizing. Make it routine; make it relaxing. As your visualization moves from the conscious to the subconscious your reality will soon follow.

SUGGESTED RESOURCES

Awaken the Giant Within: How to Take Immediate Control of Your Mental, Emotional, Physical and Financial Destiny!, by Anthony Robbins, Free Press, 1992

The Seven Spiritual Laws of Success: A Practical Guide to the Fulfillment of Your Dreams, Deepak Chopra, New World Library / Amber-Allen Publishing, 1994

Creative Visualization: Use the Power of Your Imagination to Create What You Want in Your Life, by Shakti Gawain, New World Library, Nataraj, 2002

www.dreamclinic.com

SECTION III: Compelled to Leave
Following Your Heart —
Leaving of One's Own Free Will

Many successful professionals reach a point in their careers when the challenges of the job no longer get the adrenaline pumping. Work ennui can lead to a major career overhaul, whether it is making a difference in the lives of others or being true to personal desires. Jean Godden, Janet Elliott, Gail Pettis and Sharon Giampietro are perfect examples.

When Jean joined a city newspaper in 1974, she was the second female reporter in a newsroom of eighty males. Eventually, Jean became a popular news columnist—the perfect pulpit to advocate change—but she wanted more; she wanted to make an impact not with words but with actions.

Janet wasn't planning a career change, but when IBM offered an enticing retirement package, it was too good to pass up. Now she had time to pursue her hobbies, but she still had bills to pay. How could she turn her one of her many hobbies into a money making proposition? Through her dogs, she found a way.

Gail enjoyed connecting with her patients in her growing orthodontics practice. Then she discovered jazz and began connecting with people through the world of music.

Sharon's gift with people allowed her to excel as both a social worker and then as a producer for a local television station, but neither career was a life-long fit. At age fifty, she found that her priorities had changed.

**Jean Godden's P-I beat
is offbeat Seattle.**

You've probably happened on something or someone interesting

CHAPTER IX:

Jean Godden - Choosing a Career to Make a Difference

Over twenty years ago, I sat in Jean Godden's poorly lit cubicle at the Seattle Post-Intelligencer and pitched a story to her about one of my public relations clients. She was dressed plainly in a denim skirt with the tops of her knee-high nylons peeking out underneath. She politely listened to my pitch, asked some pointed questions and included the information in her popular column, for which I was grateful. Little did I imagine that over two decades later, I would be sitting in her beautifully appointed office with an expansive view, interviewing this chic woman about her career transition at the age of sixty from newsroom to city hall.

Jean Godden wasn't born in Seattle. As the member of a military family, she lived in 116 towns and cities before taking root in this Northwest city at the age of seventeen. After two years as a journalism student at Northwestern University's Medill School of Journalism, Jean landed a summer job as the news editor at a weekly newspaper in Seattle called the *University District Herald*. It was great experience for a young journalist so Jean decided to stay at the job rather than return to school. A few years later she married, had two sons and completed her journalism degree at the University of Washington.

Upon graduating in 1974, she walked in to the newsroom of the *Seattle Post- Intelligencer* with resume in hand. Luckily, the paper was in need of a substitute for the weekly magazine editor who was on a special assignment. Jean was hired, joining a handful of women in a newsroom of almost eighty men.

Jean was soon working on the editorial page, promoted to editorial page editor and then business editor. She had been with the paper almost nine years when she was invited to write her own column. "I had never thought about being a columnist. I would be responsible for finding my own material and writing a column three or four times a week. As business editor, I was already getting home pretty late at night. This could be even worse. I asked how long I had to think about it and my boss responded, 'Take your time and tell me in the morning.'"

With encouragement from her family, Jean accepted the offer. She spent the next eight years of her career as columnist for the *Seattle P-I* and twelve with *The Seattle Times*, where, in addition to three weekday columns, she also had a treasured Sunday column that afforded her twice as many readers.

Jean enjoyed the autonomy she had as a columnist. She could select the topics she wanted to write about and even influence small changes, like the time she suggested that a large grocery chain reuse the neon sign of the popular grocery store they had replaced. By adding a few new letters to the old sign, they could retain the character of the neighborhood and still promote their brand. Her suggestion was implemented and well-received by the community.

Because Jean covered the City Hall beat, it was natural for her to think about how she would handle issues and affect change if she were in the shoes of a Seattle City Councilmember. When it came time for candidates to file for an election, she would think wistfully, "Gee, I thought someday, I might do that," and feel a little sad that her chance had passed. After all, she was nearing sixty.

As a columnist who frequently covered the local political scene, Jean kept her distance from politicians out of propriety, but she knew quite a few political consultants who would feed her information. Often when they were conducting public opinion surveys, they would add the name of a media figure into the mix to see how their candidate would fare with a popular name on the ballot. One consultant encouraged Jean to add her name into an overnight survey. The night before the filing deadline, she informed Jean that her name would do well in the polls.

Jean was convinced she had the best job in town and always assumed she would remain in journalism until retirement. But the newsroom had changed after a newspaper strike just a few months earlier—the atmosphere was a little tenser; not quite as much fun. She had lost her Sunday column and her columns were edited with a heavier hand. So in August of 2003, on the very last day a candidate could file, Jean resigned from her position at *The Seattle Times*, withdrew $850 from the bank for her filing fee and jumped into the Seattle City Council race. She got elected one hundred days later and is currently serving her second term.

When Jean compares her careers as journalist and politician she sees stark differences, as well as striking similarities. The most difficult part was learning how to become a political candidate. Once she had declared her candidacy, a fashion consultant was sent to her house and threw out her wardrobe of denim and loafers suited for a reporter. Using Jean's Nordstrom credit card, the consultant outfitted her with attire more fitting to the campaign trail and scheduled weekly appointments with a hair stylist. Her life became much more public having to frequently fill out financial reports, write her opinions on questionnaires and speak at candidate forums. As a reporter, she did some public speaking—as a politician she was expected to be fundraising. "This was the hardest part, telling people how good you are. This is absolutely the antithesis of what you were taught growing up." However, Jean learned to be quite good at it, raising almost $125,000 for her primary race and $250,000 for her campaign overall.

Jean strongly believes that the skills she acquired as a reporter, editor and columnist have helped her in her role as City Councilmember. "Like a reporter, I try to find out as much as I can on a particular topic. I talk to as many people as I can and gather as much information as possible before I vote on an issue. Fortunately, as a council member I have access to staff that can help me. I didn't have that as a journalist."

What excites Jean most about her role is her ability to influence change. "As a columnist, you can ask somebody to do something, but you don't have the wherewithal to make it happen. On the City Council,

I just need to persuade four other people." She takes great pride in her efforts to lower electric rates, advocate for library services, protect the wetlands and positively impact important social service and law enforcement programs. "As an adopted Seattleite, I really care about this city. I think that was evident during my years as a columnist, but I reached the limit of what I could do. Being on the city council has opened new doors...and I still feel like I have the best job in town."

END NOTES

Using Transferable Skills to Change Careers

You've decided it's time for a change, but what next? Do you take your valuable experience and push it aside to start all over again? Career change doesn't have to mean starting at entry level. By understanding your transferable skills, you can build on the foundation of experience you have already acquired.

Fortunately for Jean, she had a clear passion for everything Seattle. She was interested in the city's politics, businesses, people and sociology and had explored its depths through journalism. She was good at doing research, quickly grasping new and complex issues and translating them for her audience in a way that was easy to understand. Combining these skills with a desire to make Seattle the best it can be, she saw politics as a way for her to make a difference.

Identifying Transferable Skills and Interests

A popular technique used by Career Counselors to help people identify their transferable skills was developed in the 1940s by Bernard Haldane, considered to be one of the Fathers of Career Counseling. He believed people could identify their transferable skills (he called them dependable strengths) through their stories. By reflecting on positive experiences of one's past, individuals can identify skill sets used repeatedly in a variety of situations. For example, because Jean's family traveled so much, she learned to quickly orient herself to a new community by contributing stories to the neighborhood newspaper or starting a newsletter of her own. Her curiosity for new places, writing skills and ability to quickly learn "the lay of the land" were transferable skills she clearly depended on in her careers as both journalist and politician.

If you want to identify your transferable skills, take some time to reflect about your positive experience as far back as you can remember.

Think about the things you enjoyed doing, did well and made you feel proud. Perhaps it was learning to ride a two-wheeler, winning a spelling bee, organizing a softball tournament or planning your wedding. Combine work stories with personal stories and stories from childhood. Collect a minimum of ten then begin looking for patterns. Do many of your stories involve organizing events, helping others who are less fortunate, overcoming physical challenges, or creating more efficient ways of doing things? List the skills that you used in each story such as organizing, problem solving, team building or motivating. If you see these skills repeated in several of your stories, you have identified your transferable skills.

By identifying your transferable skills you can begin looking at occupations where those strengths are predominantly used and considered to be an asset by employers. For example, someone who enjoys planning parties for friends and relatives may consider a career as an event and meeting planner. If you are the person at work who always volunteers to train new employees, you may want to explore a career as a corporate trainer. Are you always creating more efficient ways to get work done? There may be a place for you in Lean Manufacturing.

A Career Counselor can help you identify occupations that may be a good fit with your list of dependable strengths. Reading job descriptions and help wanted postings will also give you a better understanding of the kind of transferable skills employers may be looking for in a particular position.

SUGGESTED RESOURCES

Career Satisfaction and Success, by Bernard Haldane, JIST, 1995

Pathfinder: How to Change Your Career for a Lifetime of Satisfaction and Success, by Nicholas Lore, Fireside, 1998

Targeting a Great Career, by Kate Wendleton, Thomson/Delmar Learning, 2006

Career Match: Connecting Who You Are with What You'll Love to Do, by Shoya Zichy and Ann Bidou, AMACOM, 2007

What Color is Your Parachute? 2010: A Practical Guide for Job Hunters and Career Changers, by Richard Bolles, Ten Speed Press, 2009

CHAPTER X:

Janet Elliott - From Passion to Paycheck

Wouldn't it be nice to get paid to read books, bake cookies or work in the garden? Many of us dream of making money from our hobbies but wonder how to make a living wage engaging in an avocation. Janet Elliott took a risk and successfully made the transition from a long-time IBM employee to making her hobby work for her.

When you walk up Janet Elliott's driveway, your first thought is that she is raising a couple of black bears in her open garage. Upon closer inspection, it is clear that the large, affable creatures you see are her Newfoundland water dogs Sidney and Casey. Large canines have always been a part of Janet's life. Growing up in Illinois, she had her St. Bernard, Putzi. In the late 1980s, she acquired Heidi, another St. Bernard who needed a home, later adding a Newfoundland to her canine family. Over the years, she competed with her dogs in water rescue, draft, agility, tracking, conformation and obedience as an active member of the

American Kennel Club. It never occurred to Janet in her thirty years at IBM that her love of dogs would one day become her work as well as her play.

Janet got her first job with IBM as a secretary supporting the marketing department soon after graduating from Miss Hickey's Secretarial School in 1964. She moved to various IBM offices in major cities such as Washington D.C., Dallas, Kansas City and Seattle. She also advanced in title and responsibility, eventually becoming a business advisor accountable for finance and sales plan exceptions.

In the early 1990s, IBM began offering employees voluntary retirement packages as a way to reduce its workforce without having to conduct forced layoffs. Although Janet qualified, she elected not to take the offer. As a single woman, she worried about her finances and how she would manage without a steady paycheck. It just seemed too risky. Therefore, she was surprised to discover that several of her mentors and many other people she respected elected to take early retirement. She decided to talk to a few of them and find out why—maybe there was something about this opportunity she had overlooked. Over dinner with a trusted colleague, she learned that in addition to a reasonable severance package, she could collect unemployment benefits because the government treated the IBM arrangement as a layoff. This unexpected source of income provided an additional incentive and Janet began thinking about life after IBM.

Janet also recalled that earlier in her career, she attended an IBM-sponsored workshop on entrepreneurship. "I don't remember much about the speaker's presentation, but two things did stick with me: First, the presenter discussed the tax advantages associated with owning your own home business. He also talked about doing something that you really love and getting paid for it. Of course, at the time I was focused on my career. But for some reason, those two pieces of advice were tucked away in the back of my mind."

Janet knew she would need a continuing source of income after leaving IBM and she began reflecting on what the speaker had said about doing what you love. She enjoyed gardening and thought about a landscape business. She also thought about doing something with photography, maybe taking pictures of people with their pets. She read literature from the Small Business Administration and went to the library to research home business opportunities.

When Janet reached the thirty-year mark in her career, IBM presented another retirement package to eligible employees. This time she decided to accept the offer. Although she wasn't quite sure how she was going to supplement her modest retirement income, she had six weeks before leaving the company to crunch some numbers and consider her next steps. She had done enough research by now to know that she had some viable options. For added security, she substantially reduced her monthly expenses by converting her fifteen-year mortgage to thirty years. And, if she needed to, she wasn't above taking on a part-time job.

Shortly before leaving IBM, a co-worker approached Janet. "I have the perfect job for you," she said. She told Janet about how she and her husband were preparing to go on vacation and had interviewed a professional pet sitter to take care of the family dogs. "We didn't really socialize at work, but everyone knew I was into dogs. Some were even envious that I was so passionate about a hobby," said Janet. "I thought about doing something with dogs, but I wasn't sure what I was qualified for. She really got me thinking about the possibilities."

Janet considered her range of options—everything from grooming, breeding, training, even pet waste removal—but pet sitting seemed to resonate with her. It was a business she could run from her home, it wouldn't require additional education or credentialing and she wouldn't need to invest much to get started. But would it make enough money to supplement her retirement income? After doing additional research at the library, she began talking to other pet sitters outside her geographic area, those that wouldn't perceive her as the competition and feel threatened by her questions. Coincidently, she did meet another businesswoman who had left her job to start a pet sitting service and seemed to be doing well financially.

Janet was somewhat reassured that her plan wasn't too far-fetched but was also warned that her time would not be her own. She would have to work weekends and holidays, the most lucrative time for pet sitters, but that part of the business didn't bother her; she was used to working "crazy hours" from her time at IBM. How she would get customers and make money is what kept her doubting. She knew pet owners weren't about to hand over their house keys and beloved pets to a stranger. She was prepared to wait table or clean houses to supplement her income while getting her business off the ground, and in fact, did a brief stint at telemarketing for some extra income.

In 1993, within a few weeks of departing IBM, Janet mustered the courage to post an ad in her community newspaper. She got two responses. The first was from a family who owned a Labrador Retriever and ended up becoming a long-term customer. The second was from an established pet sitter in the community, Annie Marx. She was working by herself and looking for someone to cover her clients in the evenings so she would be free to enjoy a social life. Annie and Janet formed an alliance. It was a great opportunity for Janet to learn the business and have the security of some guaranteed income from the beginning. In 1998, after working together for almost five years, Annie sold Janet her business. Petcetera Pet Sitting Services was launched and Janet was officially on her own.

More than a decade later, Petcetera is a thriving business and the oldest in an upscale suburb of Seattle. Although Janet occasionally does some obedience training and a little grooming, the staples of her business are feeding, walking and providing companionship to her clients' pets while they are at work or on vacation. She mainly cares for dogs and cats, but rabbits, hamsters, lizards and goldfish have also been in her charge.

Like all businesses, Petcetera has its ups and downs. On the positive side, Janet enjoys many tax advantages to owning a home business and she can dress as casually as she pleases. She feels in control of her time and has more of it to spend with her own dogs during the day. However, getting out of town is difficult, especially during the holidays. Clients can also be unreliable, calling at the last minute to say a relative will be house-sitting and her services are no longer required. "That is a hit to my pocketbook. But usually this only happens once," said Janet. "Clients realize that I have a vested interest in taking the best possible care of their pets. It's my livelihood. Most friends and relatives don't give the kind of care I provide." Sadly, on occasion, a beloved pet she has cared for over the years will die. "That is the worst part of this business. Many of my clients become friends and I really grow attached to their pets. When one dies of old age or an illness, it is very upsetting." Janet has also learned the hard way that if you are going to hire helpers, insist on a non-compete agreement, or they may walk away with your customers while they are helping you walk their dogs, as one of her trusted employees did.

How long does Janet plan to continue making a living from her fondness for four-legged creatures? "As long as I can," she responds. "As long as you are doing something you like, it really doesn't seem like work."

END NOTES

Start Out Gradually

Turning a hobby into a career is not an original concept, however most people are reluctant to do so because the earning potential is generally low, particularly when first starting out. Many people who want to profit from their hobbies will keep their day job and grow their hobby after hours. Some, like Janet, are prepared to take on a second job or start out by working for someone already in the business as they determine the best way to capitalize on their hobby.

Having an income stream you can count on, such as a steady job, will allow you to explore the marketability of your hobby to determine how to make it successful. For example, a teacher who enjoys creating textile art may sell her creations at weekend craft shows. This gives her the opportunity to understand the marketplace, how to merchandise and price her artwork and determine the type of artwork that is most popular with her customers. Gradually she may increase the number of craft shows she attends, affiliate with a gallery or sell her artwork through catalogs. In time, she has a distribution channel that will allow her to move from her classroom to her craft room full-time.

Can't Find Your Passion?

Janet was aware that many of her co-workers were envious of her passion for animals; not everyone has an obvious hobby or interest. For some of us, it takes a bit of self-discovery and creative thinking to figure out what it is we really enjoy doing and how it might relate to a new occupation. It may require visiting with a career counselor or taking career interest inventories to gain direction. There are many good books on the market devoted to helping people find their passions. *What Color is your Parachute*, by Richards Bolles, remains one of the most popular books on the market in this genre. We also highly recommend books by Barbara Sher, listed under *Suggested Resources* at the end of this chapter. Volunteering is another way to explore your interests and determine if they are worth pursuing as an occupation. Of course, don't overlook the power of brainstorming with family, friends and co-workers. Janet knew she wanted to do something with animals, but she wasn't exactly sure what that would be. She considered grooming, training and animal photography. It was a conversation with a co-worker that guided her toward pet sitting. After doing her research, Janet agreed it was a good fit and had potential to make money.

If Entrepreneurship Isn't for You

Turning a hobby or an interest into a career does not necessarily require entrepreneurship. Many people who turn a hobby into a business find they spend more time on marketing, accounting and operational tasks and less time involved in the activities that inspired them to start the business in the first place. Two young men who loved to golf started a company to help non-profit organizations raise money by organizing charitable golf tournaments. They found they were so involved in the business end of things that the only time they could actually golf was in December and January during their slow season and not an ideal time to golf in the Pacific Northwest.

Janet knew she ultimately wanted to work for herself but was grateful for the opportunity to learn the business by working as an apprentice for an established pet sitter. What if she decided she was not cut out to be in business for herself? Here are a few other scenarios Janet may have considered.

If she enjoyed sales and customer service, she could have worked in a pet store selling pet products. If she liked being around animals and handling them, she could have worked for a pet grooming service. If animal behavior interested her, she could have worked for an organization that does obedience training. An interest in animal physiology may have motivated her to return to school for training as a veterinary technician, enabling her to work in a veterinary clinic or animal hospital.

If you don't find entrepreneurship appealing, look for opportunities to work for employers that are doing business related to your interest or hobbies.

Transferring Your Skills in a New Industry

One of the easiest career transitions to make is taking the professional skills you already have and transferring them to the industry related to your special interest or passion. Perhaps you always dreamed of being a professional athlete, but weren't born with the athletic ability to get you beyond high school sports so you became an accountant. Consider using your accounting skills to work for a sports team, sports equipment or apparel manufacturer or a sports association. Perhaps you could become a sports statistician or a sports agent.

Are you a human resources professional who loves to travel? Consider looking for human resources positions with an airline, a travel agency, a tourism bureau or a large hotel chain. Are you a computer network administrator who is a nature lover at heart? Maybe a job with the US Forest Service, an environmental protection agency or a sporting goods manufacturer is right for you.

By putting your skills to work in an environment related to your special interests, you put yourself close to the action, surrounded by people that share your special interest.

You can't turn every passion into a paycheck and maybe you don't want to. If the excitement you have for your hobby starts to feel more like work you will want to take a different approach to finding a new career.

SUGGESTED RESOURCES

Wishcraft: How to Get What You Really Want, by Barbara Sher, Ballantine Books, 1979

Do What You Love and the Money Will Follow: Discovering Your Right Livelihood, by Marsha Sinetar, Dell, 1989

I Could Do Anything, If I Only Knew What It Was: How to Discover What You Really Want and How to Get It, by Barbara Sher, Delacorte Press, 1994

Work with Passion: How to Do What You Love for a Living, by Nancy Anderson, New World Library, 2004

This Time I Dance: Creating the Work You Love, by Tama J. Kieves, Tarcher, 2006

Will Work for Fun: Three Simple Steps for Turning Any Hobby or Interest into Cash, by Alan Bechtold, Wiley, 2008

Make a Living Without a Job: Winning Ways for Creating Work You Love, by Barbara Winter, Bantam, revised 2009

CHAPTER XI:

Gail Pettis - Creating a Network of Support

Gail Pettis grew up in a family of medical role models. Her father was an anesthesiologist and her grandfather and uncle were dentists. When a career counselor in high school confirmed that her interest inventory pointed to dentistry, Gail didn't think twice about her career path....until almost twenty years later.

Gail was always an excellent student, particularly in the sciences. So it was no surprise to her family or friends when she graduated from Meharry Medical College and accepted a residency in orthodontics at Harvard. Her four years of clinical training combined with research in bone biology and teaching dental students prepared her for a faculty position at the University of Tennessee in Memphis, which she accepted in 1987. For almost ten years, Gail divided her time teaching orthodontic residents, doing research and working in the faculty dental practice one day a week, the aspect of her job which she enjoyed the most.

Gail found herself being drawn to patient care full-time and thinking about private practice. Until that point, she had been committed to research and academics. She felt conflicted about which path to follow and confided in her old research advisor and long-time mentor back in Boston, Dr. Julie Glowacki, who advised Gail "to follow your heart."

In 1991, about the time Gail was considering going into private practice, she had the opportunity to attend the annual convention for the American Association of Orthodontists which was being held in Seattle. She was unable to get accommodations downtown and settled for a Bed & Breakfast at the top of Queen Anne Hill. "I got to see Seattle in a very different way than I would have had I stayed at a large hotel in the downtown core," she said. "Each day I would take the bus to and from the conference, talk with the locals and walk through the neighborhoods. I got to know Seattle in a much different way than my colleagues attending the convention, and I loved it."

Gail's enthusiasm for Seattle became a dominant topic of conversation with her colleagues back in Memphis. So much so that when an orthodontic practice was put up for sale in the Seattle area, her friends encouraged her to look in to the opportunity. Although the purchase didn't materialize, her desire to move to the Northwest increased. In 1996, Gail moved to a suburb of Seattle, found office space and opened her new orthodontic practice in the community of Issaquah.

Now a transplant with a private practice to launch, Gail was eager to make connections so she could quickly integrate into her newly-adopted community. She networked with local dentists whose patients could potentially benefit from orthodontic care. She started taking cooking classes and eventually became involved in West Coast Swing, a dance which resonated with her. Its combination of blues, jazz and funk, was the type of music Gail grew up with. Her grandfather had been a recording blues singer and guitarist and her grandmother a piano player. "I found a personal connection with this kind of music, but it was the dance that I loved. It didn't confine you to a series of steps or patterns. I loved improvising with a partner."

Gail joined the Seattle Swing Club and became very involved in dance, attending a West Coast Swing Convention in Portland and making numerous friends throughout the Northwest through a shared love of West Coast Swing. When a knee injury put a halt to Gail's new passion, she was devastated. Suddenly she was cut off from the creative expression, social interaction and physical exercise dancing provided. It created a tremendous void which she knew she needed to fill for her well-being.

During her recovery, Gail realized that she may not be able to continue dancing, but there was still the music. She heard about a jazz performance workshop and it caught her interest. In high school, she sang in the school choir and played the French horn. She also sang in church choirs and in other choral groups. Although familiar with contemporary Christian, classical music and show tunes, Gail chose jazz, the music closely aligned with the music she grew up with and to the dancing she loved. It was the right choice. In 1996, after taking a jazz workshop with Darren Motamedy, a noted jazz saxophonist, he encouraged Gail to continue her studies.

Soon Gail was taking lessons from the well-respected jazz artist and teacher Greta Matassa. She worked in her orthodontic practice during the day and participated in jam sessions at local venues at night. Although most jazz performers begin their craft at an early age, Gail's determination and innate talent allowed her to successfully transition into this difficult art form. It also didn't hurt that Seattle has a supportive community of veteran jazz artists who were generous in sharing their knowledge.

Gail's interest in the performing arts grew. Coincidentally, managing a private orthodontic practice was a responsibility that had lost its appeal. In 2006, Gail sold her practice and devoted her attention to her music full-time.

Open to opportunity, a friend introduced Gail to David Huber, a recording engineer who invited her to contribute vocals to a recording he was experimenting with. "Colabs" became a Grammy-nominated CD. Through her MySpace network, Gail made an acquaintance with Jim Martinez, who invited her to assist in teaching a workshop at the Lionel Hampton Jazz Festival in Moscow, Idaho.

Since starting her career in jazz, Gail has been artist-in-residence at the Amersfoort Jazz Festival in the Netherlands and first-place winner of the Seattle-Kobe Female Jazz Vocalist Audition. In 2007, the same year she sold her orthodontic practice, Gail released her first CD, "May I Come In?" on Origin/OA2 Records. Her second recording on the same label, "Here in the Moment," was released in January of 2010 resulting in a fourteen-week stay (peaking at #5) on the JazzWeek National Airplay Chart. Her recordings can be heard across the United States and in parts of Europe through XM Satellite Radio and Music Choice Television and she has song credits in major motion pictures.

Gail's journey from science to art may seem poles apart, but she doesn't see it that way. Both careers have required painstaking study and hard work as well as the challenges of running a business. Both careers have also allowed her personal expression, the ability to collaborate with others and to add a measure of joy into people's lives. In her first career she was designing new smiles with wires; today she is calling them forth with song.

END NOTES

Creating a Network of Support

Call it collaboration or call it networking, but you can't start a new career in a vacuum. Building on supportive relationships, finding mentors and connecting with peers creates opportunities that rarely happen on their own.

Gail created a circle of support to help her transition to a new career. Her research advisor and colleagues encouraged her to move to Seattle and start a private practice. Her jazz instructors urged her to pursue a career as a jazz singer. Club owners provided her venues to hone her craft. The performers she met along the way offered her encouragement and opportunities to contribute, in one case resulting in a Grammy-nominated CD. By surrounding herself with a community of support, Gail could tap into its collective knowledge, connections and positive energy.

Find a Mentor

A mentor is someone who can guide you along your career path. Generally, this is a relationship that has formed over time and is based on mutual respect. A mentor is different than a networking contact in that he or she has a long-term commitment in your career, offering advice and constructive criticism along the way.

Look for mentors who possess the skills you would like to develop and who are willing to share their experiences and contacts. Corporations, universities and professional associations often have formal mentorship programs and can help connect you to a mentor that is a good fit.

Ask friends for referrals. Be proactive. Mentorship relationships don't always form naturally. They require research and an effort on your part to make them happen.

Create a Network

Whether you create your community by networking on-line or face-to-face, the concept is the same: Networking is not about collecting friends; it is about establishing relationships. It should be natural and fun. When Gail moved to the Northwest, in addition to attending professional meetings to meet colleagues, she quickly joined a Swing Dance group for creative expression, physical activity and to have fun. When she could no longer dance, she discovered the jazz community. Through MySpace, a social media networking site, she was able to expand her music connections as well as her opportunities.

Think about the activities you enjoy, your special interests and the causes you care about and look for the community that is a good fit for your personality and values. Volunteering is a good place to start. Visit the Volunteer Match website (www.volunteermatch.org). Once you have made yourself open to new opportunities, they are sure to come your way.

Don't Be Afraid to Collaborate

Some people are natural joiners; others prefer to work alone. A career change is not the time to take on a Lone Ranger mentality. Creating collaborations, long or short-term, with colleagues in your newly chosen field will quickly launch you into a community vibrating with energy and possibility. For Gail, collaboration comes naturally. For, example, she has approached musicians she admires offering her lyrics for their instrumental arrangements she has heard and found enjoyable. Too often professionals in the same field see their colleagues as the "competition." However, through thoughtful collaboration, partners can learn from and play off the strengths of each other to enjoy beneficial outcomes.

SUGGESTED RESOURCES

Collaboration Handbook: Creating, Sustaining and Enjoying the Journey, by Michael Winer and Karen Ray, Fieldstone Alliance, 1994

Masters of Networking: Building Relationships for your Pocketbook and Soul, by Ivan Misner, Bard Press, 2000

Networking: Building Relationships and Opportunities for Success, by Melissa Giovagnoli and Jocelyn Carter-Millers, Jossey-Bass, 2000

Power Networking: 55 Secrets for Personal and Professional Success, by Donna Fisher and Sandy Vilas, Bard Press, 2000

Nimble Collaboration: Fine-tuning Your Collaboration for Lasting Success, by Fieldstone Alliance, 2002

The Mentee's Guide: Making Mentoring Work for You, by Lois Zachary and Lory A. Fischler, Jossey-Bass, 2005

Mentorship: A Pathway to Career Success, by Rita Boags, Authorhouse, 2008

Social Media Marketing: An Hour a Day, by Dave Eveans & Susan Bratton, Sybex, 2008

The Social Media Bible: Tactics, Tools and Strategies for Business Success, by Lon Safko & David Brake, Wiley, 2009

Volunteer Match, www.volunteermatch.org

CHAPTER XII:

Sharon Giampietro - The Art of Reinvention

Sharon Giampietro consciously chose three very different careers during her working life to enable her to capitalize on her diverse talents and interests. Whether she was using her left brain or right, each career reinvention offered its unique challenges and numerous rewards.

With a political science major and journalism minor, Sharon Giampietro unexpectedly found her first career in social services. In 1974, as an employee of Catholic Community services it was her job to help ex-offenders leaving the criminal justice system to find work. It was a job and a population she grew very fond of and it motivated her to get a Masters Degree in Social Work (MSW) from the University of Pennsylvania.

Once Sharon had her MSW, she worked in hospitals as a discharge planner and as an employee assistance professional working with hospital managers and staff regarding personal and professional issues. "What I enjoyed about social work was the interaction with people," Sharon reflected. "It was a very rewarding profession, but I also realized after almost twenty years in the job, it wasn't what I wanted to do for the rest of my life."

In 1996, Sharon decided to take a year off from work to consider her assets and her options. She was aware that she needed to hone her skills in computers, which were becoming increasingly necessary to survive in the business world, but she also wanted to revisit her interest in journalism and photography, subjects she'd enjoyed since she was a teenager.

"I was very apprehensive that year. I had left a good employer and a rewarding job without knowing what I was going to do next. But I knew I had to make a change and express another part of myself."

Sharon decided some retraining was in order and began exploring programs at community colleges. Although students of all ages are common on college campuses today, in the 1990s, Sharon, at age 46, was an oddity. Undaunted, she enrolled in three classes: Using the Internet, Photography, and Graphics for the Internet. She knew these skills would enhance her ability to get a job; she just wasn't sure what that job would be.

During a counseling session with one of the community college's career advisors, Sharon learned about an internship in the documentary department of a local television station. It piqued her interest and she applied. To her surprise, Sharon was selected for one of the five internship positions and found herself to be one of the oldest employees in a very young profession. At first her job was transcribing interviews, not exactly the creative challenge she was hoping for. When this internship was completed, she moved to another internship at the TV station — a daily show highlighting interesting stories of the local area. When this three-month internship ended, the unit manager, who valued Sharon's maturity and experience, offered her a job as a "freelancer" which eventually turned into a full time position.

"This was my first paid job in television. It was also my first awareness of how poorly the profession paid. I was working at a frantic pace for a very low wage."

Sharon excelled in her new job, eventually moving to another station where she was promoted to producer. She demonstrated excellent research capabilities and a knack for coming up with unique and creative story ideas, skills highly valued by the station managers and her associates. During her six-year career in television, working for two different stations, Sharon won three Emmys — two for stories she worked on as an Associate Producer and one for a story which she produced herself. This was quite an accomplishment for someone as new to the field as Sharon.

With Emmy's lined up on her book shelf, Sharon once again began thinking about her future. As it stood, the station recently had a reduction in its workforce. Although Sharon didn't lose her job, she was made a contract employee and lost her benefits. She still had three children in school and the hours she put in at work were long and inflexible. She would have to toil in the ranks quite a bit longer before she could hope to move to the next level as a producer again, which came with even longer hours and additional stress.

"I realized that a life in television was just too unstable. Perhaps I started too late in my career. Like social work, I loved what I was doing, but when I looked to my future, I realized I could not continue working in television until retirement."

Sharon celebrated her 50th birthday and decided it was time to prepare herself for her third and final career move. She read self-help books including Richard Bolles' *What Color is Your Parachute?*, hoping to discover her true calling. After completing the exercises in the book, all signs pointed to a career she knew she would love: a music talent scout for a major record label. "Unfortunately, it wasn't a realistic career option at my age."

As Sharon thought more about the kind of working life she wanted for herself in the future, she reflected on her past. She had worked for non-profits and in the media, which paid like non-profits. This time around she wanted a career with a flexible schedule and greater earning potential. When considering the occupations of family members, she realized that her grandfather, mother and sister-in-law had at various times enjoyed successful careers in real estate. In the past, Sharon ranked the real estate profession low in status because it didn't require a college degree. Now she started to rethink her values and her prejudices.

"At age fifty, I didn't care about career prestige so much. I was more concerned about what I could be doing until I was seventy. I knew it would take some time and a lot of hard work to build my reputation and a client base, but I had experienced my helping side and my creative side. Now I wanted to give my business side a chance."

Sharon studied for the real estate exam and, once licensed, began to talk to brokers. She eventually joined Re/Max Northwest Realtors and has been with the company for the past six years.

"I got into the business right before the real estate market peaked and had a couple of very good years. Then it hit bottom. It is a difficult but interesting business to be in right now."

Despite the challenging housing market, the effort Sharon has put into building her reputation and client base is paying off and she feels sure she will survive these tough times. It also helps that she is married to a supportive husband who happens to be an architect, a profession that is compatible with her own. In her third career reincarnation, Sharon has fashioned a vocation that suits the flexible lifestyle she desires and will allow her to work on her own terms until she chooses to retire.

"I am happy with my career choice and the decision to leave my other two careers for the real estate profession. I have moved to a spot in my personal and professional life where being my own boss is a top priority."

END NOTES

Reinvention: What to Consider

As in any long-term relationship, people either grow together or they grow apart, and a career is no different. When we are young we may value careers that allow us to advance professionally, offer new experiences, and provide monetary gain. As we get older, our values and priorities change and might no longer be compatible with our current work environment. Sharon went through this transformation twice. It wasn't about not liking her work; it was about finding work that allowed her to express different aspects of her personality and take advantage of her diverse talents.

If you want to reinvent yourself for a new career here are a few things to think about:

Capitalize on Your Strengths and Experience

You may need to go back to school to pick up a skill such as Sharon did when she took a computer class, but think carefully about going back for a college degree unless you are very certain it is required for your new profession and you are committed to the journey. Returning to school to learn a new vocation is a tremendous investment of both time and money, and you can expect to start your new career at entry level upon graduation. It may take years for you to reach an acceptable level of expertise and income.

Before each career reinvention, Sharon thought about the skills and experience she already had and how she could transfer them with a minimum amount of training. Her former journalism degree helped her get into television; she took a few classes at a community college to fill in some gaps. In real estate, she had to study several months for an exam, but the time and money she invested were minimal compared to going back for a second master's degree.

Be Mindful of Work-Life Balance

Although many people say they love to work and will do it forever, as we age some of the enthusiasm we have for full-time employment diminishes. Maybe it's our bodies telling us to slow down or the tug of those grandchildren with whom we would like to spend more time. Older workers have immense value in the wisdom of their experience and their willingness to share it with younger workers. That is why many older workers become consultants. It is a way to cash in on those years of hard work and accumulated knowledge without the stress or physical labor involved.

When Sharon was considering her third career, the balance between her work and her life was an important consideration. She wanted a job that offered her more flexibility with her time and would require less of her effort over time. In real estate, she knew she would have to work hard at first to build her referral base, but she also knew there would be a pay-off once she developed name recognition and a good reputation in the industry. At some point, she will be able to sit back and let the phone ring for her.

SUGGESTED RESOURCES

Reinventing Your Career: Surviving a Layoff and Creating New Opportunities, by Stephen Adams, Northfield Pub, 1996

Working Identity: Unconventional Strategies for Reinventing Your Career, by Herminia Ibarra, Harvard Business Press, 2004

AARP Crash Course in Finding the Work you Love: The Essential Guide to Reinventing Your Life, by Samuel Greengard, Sterling, 2008

Where to Go From Here: Reinventing – Your Career – Your Business – Your Working Life, by Douglas Campbell III, Success Coach Publishing, 2009

Coach Yourself to a New Career: 7 Steps to Reinventing Your Professional Life, by Talane Miedaner, McGraw-Hill, 2010

EPILOGUE

Terry:

Writing this book has been a transformative personal journey. Not only have I had the privilege of recording the stories of many courageous and creative career changers, but I have also had the opportunity to reflect on my own career transitions from a new perspective. I believe my need for change helped me recognize and remain open to new possibilities as well as deal with the ambiguities in a career transition. My supportive husband and network of friends allowed me to take a few calculated risks necessary to move forward. Without knowing it, I also employed many of the strategies used by the individuals interviewed and profiled for this book.

Like Peter Meeker and Robert Eich, my family had a major influence on my decision to become a teacher. I grew up in an extended family of educators who were wonderful role models and from a young age, I assumed that teaching would be my calling. I loved being in the classroom and never considered another vocation, as my Bachelors and Masters Degrees in elementary education will attest. In fact, I put my heart and soul into my work, writing out individualized lesson plans at night for each of my students, making a home visit to every student's family and signing on to teach school in the summer. It is no wonder I burned out working at this frantic pace for eight years.

When I answered a classified ad for a job with a non-profit agency writing membership publications, I only meant for it to be a one year sabbatical. I needed a break and had been doing a little freelance writing for educational publications in addition to teaching. When I joined the National School Volunteer Association in northern Virginia as their publications specialist, a whole new world opened up for me. Like most non-profits, its employees wore many hats. Soon I found myself helping to coordinate the annual membership conference, ghost-writing letters-to-the-editor for the association director, editing newsletters and pitching the media with uplifting stories about volunteerism. I didn't realize it at the time, but I was receiving on-the-job training for my next career as a public relations specialist.

It was 1982 and I was thirty-two. My sabbatical with the association was coming to an end. At the same time, my future husband proposed marriage and a move to Seattle. Career-wise, I saw this as a chance to make a clean break from the classroom and, like Jeff Levy, did some calculated risk taking. I would move to Seattle and repackage myself as a public relations professional. If that didn't work, there was always teaching to fall back on.

Luck was not with me. In 1982, unemployment in Seattle was hovering around ten percent. I was trying to break into a new profession with little experience in a market where I had no contacts. Like Harvey Nagle, I was willing to try anything. I picked up some pro bono work publicizing a few fledgling businesses and a couple of charity auctions. I wasn't collecting a paycheck but, in the manner of Gail Pettis, I was creating a network of support and valuable contacts. After a year of cold calling, resume writing, informational interviewing and relationship building, I was able to convince the general manager at Ogilvy & Mather Public Relations to hire me as a "paid intern" for three months. I would get agency experience and they would benefit from the media contacts I had made over the last year. At the end of my internship, I was hired as a full-time public relations specialist responsible for clients such as Westin Hotels, Roman Meal Bread and Chateau St. Michele Winery. I am convinced it was the volunteer experience, the networking contacts, and persistence, that got me the job.

With seven years in a PR agency under my belt, I stumbled upon another classified ad for a PR/Marketing Director at a local hospital. I wasn't actively seeking a new job but this looked interesting. Once I submitted my resume, I promptly forgot about the position until I received a call a few months later for an interview. In January 1991, after a series of twelve interviews over the course of several months, I was hired as the Director of Marketing/Public Relations for a suburban hospital and medical center. It was to be my home for the next eleven years.

As the Marketing/PR Director I sat on the executive team. It was exhilarating and extremely challenging work. I had quite a bit of creative freedom, learned how to manage a staff and enjoyed executive retreats at fashionable resorts. I was also at the behest of a marketing savvy CEO, who when inspired, would call at all hours during evenings and weekends to share his thoughts and dole out assignments which made me feel important, for the first few years anyway.

By the late 1990s, my enthusiasm for my work was waning and the office politics were not to my liking. My intuition told me I needed a change, but I wasn't sure what that should be. Did I need a new job or a new career? Unhappy and confused, I sought the advice of a professional career counselor.

I found the Myers Briggs Type Inventory and other personality assessments interesting, but not very useful. Mainly, they were validation that I had been in appropriate careers for my temperament. Teacher and public relations specialist reappeared on each list. What I did find helpful was the suggestion from my counselor to explore the extension programs offered by the University of Washington. She recommended two programs — Training Specialist and Career Development Facilitator (CDF). Since the closing date for the latter was quickly approaching, I applied for the Career Development Facilitator program first, and was immediately accepted. Like Sharon Giampietro, I found myself back in school at the age of fifty, only now I was working full-time at the hospital and trekking up the I-5 corridor during rush hour once a week for the next nine months to the University of Washington Seattle campus. It was painful, but it was temporary. I could do this.

Through the exercises in the CDF program, it became clear that a career as a Career Development Facilitator was the perfect next step for me. It combined my love of teaching with the creativity of marketing to teach people how to market themselves for employment. Still, I wasn't exactly sure how I would be compensated for this type of work. I could work in the career center of a high school or college, but that would mean starting over again at an entry level wage. Perhaps I should work in an employment agency. After job shadowing at a local staffing agency for half a day, the answer was clearly "No." Providing outplacement counseling for businesses conducting layoffs appealed to me but the major companies offering that service didn't hire staff, they hired consultants on an as needed basis. Did I want to be a self-employed contractor? Maybe.

I worked another year at the hospital in my role as Marketing/PR Director. My evenings and weekends were spent volunteering at Youth and Family Services where I created a small career library and helped clients with resume writing and job search strategies. I was gaining the confidence and experience needed to go into a private practice. Next I went to my boss and renegotiated my role at the hospital. Since managers weren't allowed to work part-time, in 2002, I stepped down from my management position and created a three-day a week "bridge" job fundraising for specific hospital programs. This wasn't a job I relished, but it allowed me to work part-time and build my career counseling practice...and my cash flow. On my days off, I conducted job finding workshops for a national outplacement firm on a contract basis or met one-on-one with clients who had heard about me through word-of-mouth.

Through strategic networking and my willingness to take on almost any assignment or client, I had developed a portfolio career with multiple income streams similar to John Curley. With a few contracts and sub-contracts in my portfolio, it was time to part ways with the hospital. I was officially in private practice full-time as a career consultant and coach.

These past ten years have been filled with many rewards and a few surprises. I never anticipated teaching job search skills to a room of ex-offenders, which I do four days each month as a sub-contractor for the County. It is one of my favorite assignments. Nor did I consider becoming a telecoach until I joined the Five O'clock Club and conducted job search support groups once a week by phone to job seekers around the country. For nine months I worked with newly graduated MBA students at the University of Washington career center as a part-time adjunct employee. I also learned a great deal about building airplanes having written hundreds of resumes for Boeing employees as one of their designated resume writing vendors. Another aspect of my job is providing employment assistance to the spouses of corporate employees who are newly relocated to Washington State. This was a new twist on career counseling that I hadn't expected.

When David Lingle approached me about this book, I had just authored a series of e-books on career issues for a publisher called Get-to-the-Point Books. His timing was perfect; I had been taking an on-line course in creative non-fiction and this project renewed my interest in writing. I saw David's proposal as an opportunity to further my professional development, enhance my work with my clients and pursue my personal interest in writing.

I still love my work as a career counselor, but in the back of my mind I keep thinking about Janet Elliott. Perhaps I too can turn my writing hobby into a paycheck. Is there another career in my future? After all, I am only sixty and still have a few good careers in me.

David:

I lost 60 percent of my team in December 2008. At the time, I was the software development manager for a health care company. The timing and severity of the layoff was unexpected, and this act made the inevitable demise of the company certain. It was my triggering event. After overcoming the shock and figuring out what I could do with the remainder of the team, I realized that it was time for me to think about a new career.

Changing careers was not a new concept for me. My first career change came in 1990 when I was teaching computer science at a university and realized that I wanted to practice the subject rather than teach it. I left the university to become a software engineer. Although the nature of my work and responsibilities changed, it was not a complete break from the past as there is a common foundation to both professions. At the time I thought that I would write code forever. This lasted ten years.

"Never get out of the boat" is a famous quote from the movie *Apocalypse Now*. For programmers, the analogy is "Never leave the code." Programming is a skill that takes practice and dedication. Once stopped it is difficult to start again with the same intensity. Nevertheless, a typical career path is from developer to manager and I was on that trajectory. I quickly learned that it is very difficult to be a manager and a programmer simultaneously; one or the other suffers. Eventually I chose to commit to being a manager, leaving my programming skills behind.

During a meeting with the executive team of a web-based start up, I listened to a discussion of how we should market our product. I was incredulous as to some of the things that were being said about target audiences and market share. "How do these people know this?" I asked myself. All of my training had been technical. If I were going to participate at this level in an organization, I needed to learn about business. In 2004, I graduated from the Executive MBA program at the University of Washington. The course of study, my fellow students, and the community around the program did more than teach me about business. I started to wonder about career possibilities in fields that I had never before considered.

Four years later, with a severance notice in my hand, it was time to take the seeds that had been germinating in my mind and turn them into a concrete vision of a new career. Fortunately, from the time the layoff was announced until my job officially ended, I had some leeway to plan for a new career. I was open to making a complete change, but the transition to something different was more difficult than the changes I had made in the past, and I was at a loss as to where to begin. It occurred to me that the best way to find out how to make a career change was to talk to others who had done it. I knew that I needed help in this project, and I asked Terry if she was interested. Fortunately she was, and we began listening to and questioning those who had successfully changed careers.

The most difficult part of my career search has been the ambiguity of what I will do next. When there are an infinite number of possibilities there are really none. I am comforted that I am not alone in this feeling as it was common to most of the people we interviewed. As frustrating as it is, I am encouraged because I know it is part of a process. Following techniques mentioned in the stories, I re-evaluated my interests, skills, passions and goals and investigated options I would never have considered in the past, such as owning a franchise or working for the post office. Although the fog hasn't quite lifted, I am becoming clearer about the attributes I do and don't want for my next career.

Networking and having a support group played a large role for all of our career changers. Over the last year, I have worked on expanding my community. I have been in touch with friends and co-workers from my past and made new connections. I have joined professional groups and took on the role of volunteer mentor for a local university. Each connection has led to another, and my community has expanded two-fold. I am fortunate to have the encouragement and support from my family and friends as I explore new possibilities.

As we learned from the people we interviewed, there are risks to any significant change. Knowing how others were able to evaluate risk in the formulation of their plans to make a career change has helped me deal with my own concerns. A plan provides us with a goal, but does not preclude experimentation. The degree of uncertainty is large at first but narrows over time as we evaluate and reject alternatives to reaching that goal. As I consider new career options, I have learned to evaluate the risks, create worst case scenarios and ask myself, "What are the consequences if I fail?" At times, I am tempted to get another job in software development because it is what I know. But I am also much more confident about looking outside my comfort zone, knowing how to evaluate the level of risk.

Branch Ricky, a baseball executive, once said, "Luck is the residue of design." We assess ourselves and make plans, but we should be aware of the hints and clues that come our way. This is the role that serendipity plays in a career change. It can happen when we are waiting out a rain storm in a bookstore and see a book on franchising or it can happen when a homeless person crosses the road in front of us and strikes a chord in our heart. I have not quite reached my goal, but I am certain I am on the same path shared by the successful career changers we profiled. With an open heart and mind for any hints and clues that may come my way, I await the next opportunity.

For more information or to contact Terry and David go to:

Restart Enterprises LLP
www.restartenterprises.com
restartenterprises@gmail.com

Or

Terry Pile – terryp@careeradvisorsonline.com
David Lingle – restartenterprises@gmail.com

Terry Pile, MS, GCDF
Career Consultant and Coach
terryp@careeradvisoronline.com

Terry started her private practice, Career Advisors, in 2000. She is president of Restart Enterprises, the resource for mid-life career changers. Terry has a master's degree in education from Indiana University and a certificate in career development from the University of Washington. She is certified by the Center for Credentialing and Education as a Global Career Development Facilitator (GCDF). In addition, to consulting and training, Terry writes occasional feature articles on career issues for newspapers and e-zines. She has published five electronic books on career topics through Get to the Point Books, www.gettothepointooks.com

David Lingle, MA, MS, MBA
restartenterprises@gmail.com

After careers as a soldier, educator, and software developer, David is currently CEO of Restart Enterprises, a resource for mid-life career changers. He has contributed to the success of large companies such as Hewlett-Packard as well as holding leadership positions at two Seattle area start-ups, Isilon Systems and Appliant. David earned bachelors and master's degrees in mathematics from Southern Illinois University and a master's degree in computer science from The State University of New York at Stony Brook. He graduated in 2004 with an MBA from the University of Washington's Executive MBA program.